MOMMY IQ

MOMMY IQ

The Complete Guide to Pregnancy

rosie pope

FOREWORD BY DR. AMOS GRUNEBAUM

itbooks

AN IMPRINT OF HARPERCOLLINSPUBLISHERS

This book is written as a source of information about all aspects of pregnancy. It is based on the research and observations of the author, who is not a medical doctor. All pregnant women should be under the care of a qualified medical professional, and the information contained in this book should by no means be considered a substitute for the advice of that professional.

The information in this book has been carefully researched, and all efforts have been made to ensure accuracy as of the date published. The author and the publisher expressly disclaim responsibility for any adverse effects arising from the use or application of the information contained in this book.

FIRST EDITION

Library of Congress Cataloging-in-Publication Data

Pope, Rosie.
    Mommy IQ : the complete guide to pregnancy / Rosie Pope ; foreword by Amos Grunebaum.
        p.   cm.
    Includes index.
    ISBN 978-0-06-219260-8 (pbk.)
    1. Pregnancy—Popular works.   2. Childbirth—Popular works.   3. Pregnant women—Health and hygiene—Popular works.   I. Title.
    RG551.P67 2012
    618.2-dc23   2012019238

12 13 14 15 16   DIX/RRD   10 9 8 7 6 5 4 3 2 1

To my Nana, whose spirit has always
and will always inspire me.

To my husband, whose unwavering support
has made this all possible.

To my children, for teaching me every day
how to be a better mom.

contents

FOREWORD

Dr. Amos Grunebaum

I knew I wanted to be around babies from the time I was five years old. Growing up in Cologne, Germany, I often accompanied my father, a professional photographer, as he took pictures of newborns in the local hospital. It was when I was at his side, snapping close-ups of new babies, that I was inspired to become an obstetrician.

In my experience, obstetrics is the most exciting medical specialty. Pregnancy and childbirth are two of the most amazing things that happen in this world—and who wants a boring job? Just think: over the course of nine months, a woman can turn just two tiny cells into a thriving, breathing baby—or two, or sometimes more. My respect for women and mothers increases with each delivery I perform. I love the passion and thought women bring into their pregnancies—yes, even when those passions and thoughts result in 3 a.m. phone calls.

The other reason I'm a doctor? I am a child of the 60s and grew up with the Rolling Stones, the Beatles, the Kinks, the Who, and Bob Dylan. For a very short time I played bass in a local rock group. I loved being on stage, but it quickly became apparent that I was tone-deaf and a terrible singer. Naturally, the next best thing was to become a doctor. The British term for an operating room is the "operating theatre," so I found another opportunity for performing—no singing required. I do enjoy returning to my musical roots, though, even if I never made it as a rock star; as long as it makes my patients comfortable, I now play music during deliveries, and my preferred song is "Beautiful Day" by U2.

Over the last 30-plus years, I have delivered over 3,000 babies. And still, each and every time I take care of a pregnant woman and deliver her baby, I am amazed. Each experience is different. With today's technology, many details of a pregnancy can be predicted ahead of time, such as the baby's sex, weight, and other physical characteristics. But there is still one mystery that is only revealed when the baby emerges from the uterus: the child's hair color. At the present time, there is no medical test in the world that can determine the hair color ahead of the delivery. When my daughter Emma was born with a shock of red hair, not only were we happy that she was healthy, we reveled in the beauty of her unique appearance. It may seem like a small detail, but it goes to show you there will always be an element of surprise in the delivery room.

I also enjoy being an obstetrician because I find that pregnant women exemplify selflessness, something many people believe has disappeared from our culture. I have the great privilege of witnessing a pregnant woman's selflessness every day. A mother-to-be needs and deserves to be fully informed about what is happening both to her body and her baby. She needs the freedom to make smart, informed, and often selfless decisions for her family based on that information.

Many pregnant women are reluctant to ask their doctor too many questions. But remember—doctors are not mind readers. Don't be afraid to ask about the issues that concern you. Any good doctor will welcome your questions with open arms—especially because sometimes the smallest concerns, the ones you think are probably nothing, may need medical attention right away. For this reason, I openly encourage my patients to ask me every question they can think of, and I encourage them to do it the modern way: by email. However, I do admit, there are some questions I may not be able to answer—like who will win next year's Super Bowl. You might want to ask Rosie's husband about that one.

Which brings me to Rosie herself. I delivered Rosie's three children. Rosie has asked more questions than almost any mother I've ever met—because she knows she's not just asking them for herself, she is asking them for all of you mothers-to-be out there! Rosie is adamant that every mother deserves the highest quality of care and the most thorough, up-to-date information at every step along the way, but she has also maintained a real sense of wonder about pregnancy and delivery—despite having already gone through the whole process three times. I knew from the moment Rosie mentioned the idea for this book that it would really speak to the women I see every day in my office: women who are busy, ambitious, with a full plate of responsibilities, and who are both overjoyed and sometimes a bit scared about their transition to motherhood—women who need the facts, but who also need a friendly guide through this period of change, excitement, and hope.

My prescription for all women who are pregnant or trying to conceive is to have Rosie Pope in their lives. However, because she is only one woman—and because I think her family would miss her quite a lot if she spent all her time with my patients—I will instead prescribe this book to you.

Among Rosie's wisdom on in-laws, due-date anxiety, and, yes, even fashion, you will find the same up-to-the-minute medical information and statistics that I give my patients as Director of Obstetrics and the Chief of Labor and Delivery at the New York Weill Cornell Medical Center. My hope is that this information will make you feel more confident and sure of yourself as you progress throughout your pregnancy.

This book is by no means intended to be a replacement for a strong, communicative relationship with your doctor, but as a companion to your journey, one that will help you learn and perhaps laugh a little, too. I wish you all the best of health in your pregnancy.

A NOTE FROM ROSIE

Hey there! Whether you're trying for a baby, you're already a mommy-to-be, or you're a full-fledged mama getting ready to welcome another new member to your family, welcome! I'm so excited, and honestly humbled, to play a part in your pregnancy journey. To start things off, I want to take a minute to explain why I've written this book. Sure, it's my job to help women enjoy a happy, healthy pregnancy—and of course I wanted to share everything I know—but the real reason is because I've been in your fabulous shoes before. I don't often tell the story of my oldest son, J. R.'s, first (absolutely crazy!) 72 hours of life because I think it makes me seem like a really clueless mom. But the thing is, I *was* kind of a clueless mom back then—I didn't have the slightest idea as to how to be a good one . . . *yet*.

Let's go back to Labor Day weekend 2008. We'd been hearing rumblings that the firm where my husband worked, Lehman Brothers, was about to go bankrupt, the contractor I'd hired to build my first Rosie Pope Maternity boutique in New York was way behind schedule (the store was due to open just after Labor Day weekend), and, um, I was carrying a baby on the brink of arrival. Daron and I were home in our New York City apartment when I realized my minute-long contractions were coming every five minutes—exactly what the doctors had said would signal the start of labor. Everything around us may have been chaos, but I was determined that my son would have a perfect birth. I cruised into the bathroom, gave myself a mini-blowout and put on fresh makeup

(I *knew* those delivery room photos would end up online), and packed a massive bag full of crime novels to help me pass the time before and after the big moment—of course I thought I'd have free time on my hands (so sweet and innocent in retrospect!).

Cruising to the hospital on the FDR Drive, Daron cranked up Justin Timberlake's "Sexy Back," and I couldn't stop thinking we could take on the world. I felt better than fine, delivery was going to be a piece of cake, and we were going to be the coolest, most gorgeous family ever. Cuter than Tori and Dean, hotter than Brangelina, with everything under control and gobs of time for catching up on books.

When we got to the hospital, a steely-faced nurse met us at the desk and asked what we needed. When I told her I was there to have my baby, she just stared at me, shook her head, and said, "You're not ready," before sending us on our way. Back at home, I collapsed in a pile on the pristine white shag rug I'd chosen for the nursery—the oh-so-practical fibers already getting matted from my tears. Couldn't the nurse see that my contractions were textbook? Now I was going to have to give birth in my apartment, which would make a huge mess for when company came over to visit—not to mention the fact that we had no idea how to deliver a baby on our own. To be plain, I was a little freaked out and a lot pissed.

Fast-forward four hours and dial my pain level up to eleven. With not-so-freshly applied mascara streaking down my face and my hair almost as ratted as that shag rug, I screamed for Daron to get the car. Off we went again, this time without my bag of books, without a change of clothes, and without a clue as to what we were in for. Back at the hospital, the same nurse greeted us at reception. She gave me the biggest hug. "Oh, honey," she said, "*now* you're ready."

After about 26 hours of craziness—including four hours of pushing that caused the blood vessels in my eyes to pop so that I looked like I'd been in a boxing match—I finally got to hold my precious son. Holding him, I really understood for the first time that he would always come before me, and that I wanted it that way. His little bottles of baby shampoo would take priority over my salon appointments and I would do anything, really *anything*, to make sure he was happy and healthy.

Just days after we got home, my husband had to go back to Lehman Brothers to clean out his desk, and I was set to take our son to his first doctor's appointment. I was determined to give our precious boy a stylish debut, so despite the 98-degree weather I swaddled him in a super-luxe cashmere set and started to set him into his stroller. That's when it happened—a slight thud, followed by a sharp cry let me know I'd banged my baby's head on the stroller bar. Convinced I'd given him irreversible brain damage, and in an obviously irrational state, I decided I should hit my own head against the same bar as hard as I could—so that I could feel what he might be feeling. Conclusion? My head *really* hurt, so his must, too.

I called Daron in hysterics and he rushed over to drive us to the appointment—which was a mere five-minute walk away, I might add! The doctor took one look at the three of us, told me to ditch the cashmere baby clothes until winter, and said that although the baby was fine, I had given myself a full-blown concussion and she was concerned with how *I* was coping!

I wouldn't be shocked if a Google search for "massive stress ball" resulted in a photo of me in my first days of mommyhood. Not that I didn't try to prepare myself, mind you. I'd read all the traditional medical guides on pregnancy leading up to that fateful Labor Day, but if I'd had a book more like *Mommy IQ*—a book that fit my busy lifestyle and that spoke to me as a *woman*—I know I would have felt less alone and better prepared for the real-world situations I'd be going through. Not to mention that my poor little firstborn wouldn't have had to deal with a concussed mom his first week out of the womb!

I've come a long way since my oldest child's homecoming, and I have gained an immense amount of wisdom from my profession and the medical and lifestyle experts on my MomPrep Expert Panel. In fact, I've boosted my own Mommy IQ to levels that helped me give birth to my second son in 2011 and my third child earlier this year without a hint of drama *or* head trauma. My access to top-notch specialists is exceptional, but I don't think it *should* be. *Mommy IQ* is my way of sharing what I've learned (mainly the hard way!) with you, in a book that I wish I'd had to guide me years ago.

The Very Beginning
from trying to peeing on a stick

Mommy IQ:

What you'll be figuring out this month

- ○ The best (and worst) tricks for getting pregnant

- ○ When to see a pro

- ○ How to know you're pregnant without consulting a Ouija board

- ○ The at-home test

- ○ Newsflash: coffee doesn't count as breakfast

- ○ Pills to pop—and what to stop

- ○ I have rights, don't I? Figuring out maternity leave

- ○ Hunting for doctors

- ○ What's a tribe?

- ○ Murmurs from the Man Cave

{ My **Mommy IQ** is ___ out of 10 }

I've pretty much covered the gamut when it comes to getting pregnant. I've had one too many martinis, fallen into bed with my husband, and gotten pregnant. I've taken a full regime of fertility medications and had to undergo IVF (in vitro fertilization for those of you newbies out there!). I've had an ectopic pregnancy and fallopian tube removal; and finally, I've gotten pregnant when no one said it was possible. There are *so* many ways to create a baby, and the truth is that it simply *won't matter* which one got you there once you've got a thriving baby sleeping in your arms.

The moment you decide to become a mom, you're forced to grow up a little—you're preparing for the most selfless time of your life, because no decision made in parenting should be self-indulgent. Suddenly you're faced with hundreds of decisions, big and small, that will affect you, your family, and the little one who will soon look to you for *everything*. Don't panic. I'm here to help with all of that, and to give you the information you need to make the best choices for you and your family every step of the way.

So whether you're still trying to get pregnant (the old-fashioned way or any other way, for that matter) or have just found out you're expecting, take a minute now to think about how amazing this whole journey will be—and also try to realize (and learn to be okay with!) the idea that many things will be out of your hands. As much as you research and plan, make choices and prepare, you just can't control the how or why or when of *every* aspect of your pregnancy. That said, you can put yourself in the healthiest place to be an amazing parent, both while you're trying to conceive and in pregnancy.

Parenthood itself is a lifelong experiment in adjustment and flexibility in the face of the unexpected, and I really believe that the process of getting pregnant—even if there are unforeseen hurdles—prepares you for the vast array of experiences ahead of you. Be patient and take joy in surprises. I'm so excited for your journey to unfold!

Rosie's maternity mantras

Hello, hello! If you're reading this, it means you've either decided to become a mommy or you're already on your way. (And if you're already pregnant? *Don't skip this chapter.* There's lots of good stuff in here that you'll need in order to get up to speed.)

As I've said, pregnancy can be a long road, with tons of ups and downs along the way, so it's important to keep a sense of humor and have a little fun with it whenever you can. To help, I'll have some deep thoughts to share at every major point in your journey. For our first maternity mantra, I've got a bit of wisdom for you from one of the greatest minds of all time, followed by a good, old-fashioned truth (if you can call it that!) from one of the most notorious philosophers of reality TV.

> " It is said that the present is pregnant with **the future.**"
>
> —VOLTAIRE, WRITER, HISTORIAN, AND PHILOSOPHER

> " Whoever I have babies with **has to be Italian.** I want my kid's last name to have a vowel on it . . . and be tanned, **obviously.**"
>
> —SNOOKI, *JERSEY SHORE*

The best (and worst) tricks for getting pregnant

Oh baby! Getting pregnant can be so easy—and, let's admit, a lot of fun—for one woman, and a whole lot of effort, struggle, and sadness for another. I've been on both sides of that coin, and while I hope that you don't have to retrace all the steps my husband and I had to go through, I will say I'd do it all again if I had to, and probably even more, if that's what it took to have my wonderful children at my side.

My point is that when you want a baby, you're pretty much willing to try any trick of the trade, no matter if you heard it from the nutso lady at your corner bagel shop or from your own mother. "Wait, you said I'll get pregnant if I eat a fried egg with hot sauce on the night of the full moon? On it!" The anticipation of becoming a parent is enough to drive even the most rational of us a little batty. Here, I've rounded up the best, most reliable baby-making techniques—and a few that you shouldn't waste your time on. Trust me. I may have tried them all (*shhh!*).

DO stop taking birth control pills, or stop using other hormone-based birth control methods, a few months before you might want to get pregnant. It's a myth that it's not possible and not safe to get pregnant for two to three months after stopping, so go ahead and start trying right away. It just might take a few months for your ovulation cycle to get back to normal.

DON'T get totally drunk before cuddling with your guy, and the same goes for him. Excessive alcohol can actually lower your chances of conceiving—something that makes a ton of sense to me. I mean, if I've had a tad too many cocktails, my husband pretty much has to guide me home—so you can't blame a sperm and egg from missing each other under the same circumstances!

DO try to have sex two to three times a week. A little bedroom action every couple of days isn't just fun—it makes it almost impossible for you to miss a fertile period.

DON'T feel like you have to do it every night. If you're too tired, and he's too tired, and you're flopping around like fish out of water, it just kind of takes the joy out of it. Besides, stress and fatigue can affect fertility. You don't want to mess with that.

DO use the little ovulation sticks that come in ovulation predictor kits. They'll tell you when your luteinizing hormones are surging, which coordinates with your most fertile time—right before ovulation. The sticks are way easier and more dependable than tracking your period on a calendar, and who has the time for all that anyway?

DON'T freak out if you can't have sex right at the exact moment when you think you're most fertile. Getting pregnant is supposed to be the fun part, remember? Have sex because you want to, not just because you want a baby. And if one of you is on a business trip or has the flu when your ovulation sticks say it's time to go to it, don't get too stressed and let it turn into an argument. Getting pregnant might be easy or difficult, but either way your partner is on this team with you as the future role model, mentor, and hero to your little one, not just someone you need there when you're ovulating!

SMART BITS

I know how sacred your schedule is, because mine is just as important to me. I make schedules for work, for meeting up with friends, for workouts, for naptimes, for dinnertimes, and I've even been known to schedule in time to make schedules—no joke! I think I drive my husband crazy with all of my scheduling, but it's the only way I know to get everything done.

But babies? Well, they just don't work on our timelines. It is exceptionally difficult to get pregnant *exactly* when you want. In fact, the average healthy couple under 35 can take up to a year to conceive. So if it's not happening right away, try not to sweat it, and enjoy not being pregnant for the time being. These are the last moments of your life when you get to focus on just you—so rock your skinniest jeans, stay out late with the girls, and indulge a little.

Having said that, I have been through infertility and know that it can be virtually impossible to relax when things aren't going as planned. But you must find a way to cope, and distraction is sometimes your best defense. Of course it's annoying to hear that you need to focus on other things, but I'm only telling you that because I know it helps. You will find your family—it's the when and how that are often a surprise.

When to see a pro

For lots of us, it's not as simple as a fun night out, a little dancing in the kitchen, and then *bada-bing-bada* . . . baby! Getting pregnant can be quite tricky, frustrating, and even scary at times, but having a specialist on your side can make life a lot more bearable—and it can majorly increase your chances of conceiving. If you're over 35, know there are fertility issues in either your family history or your partner's, have been diagnosed with polycystic ovarian syndrome (one of the most common fertility issues in women), or have been trying to conceive for more than a year, it is time to seek out a professional. Women most commonly seek out a reproductive endocrinologist, a doctor who can help with your overall fertility, but a urologist can also check into your guy's swimmers (and make sure they don't need a few lessons in the deep end!). If you've got deeper medical issues at play, the reproductive endocrinologist might refer you to a reproductive surgeon who can help you become more fertile through further medical procedures—depending of course on your specific case.

The bummer here is that fertility specialists of any kind can be spendy, and not all insurance companies cover them or the tests and procedures they might offer. Definitely call your insurance company first and look into plans that offer some coverage before jumping in. Fertility docs really can turn the Ovulation Olympics into a baby boom, but nobody wants to end up with unexpected bills that they can't afford. Resolve.org, the website of the National Infertility Association, provides information on grants, scholarships, and other financial aid for infertility treatments that might be too expensive for your household. Go to their site to learn more.

PAGING DR. GRUNEBAUM

Even with all of my own crazy experience in pregnancyland, and after helping hundreds of clients through their own journeys, I am the first to admit that while I may be an expert, I am *not* a doctor! There are so many things that I can feel sure of only after hearing them from a doctor, and I'm sure you feel the same way—which is why I've asked my phenomenal doctor, Dr. Amos Grunebaum, to help me answer some of the toughest medical questions about pregnancy throughout this book.

Dr. Grunebaum is not only my own personal doctor—and the man responsible for delivering each of my gorgeous children (along with more than 3,000 others in his career!)—but, as the director of Obstetrics and chief of Labor and Delivery at the New York-Presbyterian Hospital/Weill Cornell Medical Center (one of the top hospitals in the U.S.), he is also one of the top doctors in the *nation*. Beyond knowing the facts and keeping up with all the latest research, Dr. Grunebaum is an all-around terrific guy who loves women, loves babies, and wants every pregnancy to be as healthy and happy as possible. I hope you'll find his insights just as helpful as I always do.

Now, without further adulations of Dr. Grunebaum (I could really go on all day—it's hard not to when he's been such a part of helping me grow my family!), here's the first big question for him:

Who should see a fertility specialist, and how do you know if there's a problem?

The traditional diagnosis of infertility is usually made after unsuccessfully trying to conceive for more than one year—so that's usually the time that most couples would seek help. But Rosie's family is living proof that being diagnosed with infertility doesn't mean you can't get pregnant! Many couples who have been trying to get pregnant *will* successfully conceive later on, especially if they have help from a professional.

Still, not everyone should wait a full year before seeing a specialist. The American Society for Reproductive Medicine (ASRM) suggests that couples in which the woman who is trying to get pregnant is over the age of 35 should seek help after six months of trying. And couples who have known causes of infertility should seek help even sooner, regardless of the mother's age. These include couples with endometriosis, fibroids, irregular periods, prior abortion, exposure to diethylstilbestrol, varicoceles, prior cancer treatment, and those about to undergo chemotherapy. If you fit into any of these categories, definitely reach out and find a good reproductive specialist who can help you.

How to know you're pregnant without consulting the Ouija board

To put it bluntly, baby lust can make you a little delusional. It's easy to believe that just because you want a tiny babe so badly, and because you quit the pill last week and have had sex *twice* since then, of course you're pregnant! Once you start looking up early pregnancy symptoms on the Web, it's tempting to fudge the date of your last period to figure out when your baby *would* be due if you *were* pregnant, and then you figure out the baby's would-be star sign, and before you know it, you're *convinced* that there's already a little baby growing in there.

In case you can't tell, I've totally been there—the crazy lady on the baby sites at 3 a.m., convincing myself that I was pregnant. For your convenience, I've listed a few common things you might be feeling right now and decoded their true meanings below, because, well, early signs of pregnancy really can be something else entirely, or of course, you really *could* be pregnant.

Basically, love, until you pee on that stick and the pregnancy test tells you you're pregnant, try, try, *try* not to analyze every symptom. It'll just make the days seem like years. Hang in there and don't give up hope. The waiting—and hoping and praying and wanting and wishing—really is the hardest part. When the time is right, everything will fall into place for you.

The at-home test

I know the feeling. You just *really* want to know if you're pregnant. And those at-home pregnancy tests are so easy to just pick up at the market—almost *too* easy, in fact. After you do the first test, it's hard to not be hooked. Soon, you're finding yourself trying one in the bathroom at work on your lunch break, or in the ladies' room when you're out to dinner with the girls.

if you feel ...	it could be ...	or maybe ...
like your jubblies* have tripled in size and your nipples are sensitive	that you shrunk your shirts in the laundry again	**you're pregnant!**
super tired and a little out of sorts	that Starbucks screwed up this morning and gave you a decaf	**you're pregnant!**
like you've gotta have doughnuts and peanut butter and Swiss cheese sandwiches all at once	because those things taste good together	**you're pregnant!**
super-nauseated	because you ate doughnuts and peanut butter and Swiss cheese sandwiches all at once	**you're pregnant!**

Every time I did an at-home test and it came out negative, I had that sinking feeling and wondered "Why not yet?" and, even worse, "Why not *me*?" Save yourself a little heartbreak (and some cash—you can spend a bundle on those things before you realize it!) and just take the test when you think you *really* could be pregnant—like the first day of your missed period. And make sure to read the instructions. In the excitement of wanting to rip open the box and pee on the thing, it's easy to toss aside that little folded piece of paper, but it's important that you take the two seconds to know what you're doing. False negatives are actually pretty common with at-home testing, and that can be because overanxious moms-to-be (I think that means all of us!) think we know how to work these things when maybe we really don't!

Once you're at the rational testing point, there's another challenge: peeing on a stick is actually *tricky*. How much should you pee on it? What if you're not getting the right result because you didn't pee on it enough? Should you pee on it *again*? You can skip the whole ordeal of precision peeing by just peeing into a disposable cup, and then sticking the test directly into it. I think you'll find that to be much easier.

Another note on those false negatives we talked about a bit ago—if you aren't convinced that your at-home test was reliable, call your doc, make an appointment, and get a blood test done. It's the most authoritative answer. Doctors can often get the results back to you that same day, and if not, then early the next. Trust me—I know how excruciating the waiting can be.

> *** Rosie, Decoded**
>
> **Jubblies: (*noun, plural*):** It's the nicest word I can think of for your breasts; less clinical than chest or breasts, totally not rude like boobs or, God forbid, tits. Your grandmother could comment on your lovely jubblies, and it would be fine—in fact, mine did.

SMART BITS

When that stick finally does show you that little "Yay, you're pregnant!" line (or two lines, or a plus sign—as I said, read the directions!), it might be hard to contain your joy, but be careful what you do next. A used pregnancy test is not exactly the kind of thing you want to wave around in people's faces. To you that stick might be an affirmation, a reminder that that little babe is the real deal now—but to friends, coworkers, neighbors, and maybe even your partner, it's a plastic stick that you *peed* on! I completely understand keeping it tucked away for a little while in the medicine cabinet, but there's no need to frame it in the living room next to Grandma Ethel or to bring it along to your next girls' outing. I mean, you don't show your old toilet paper to friends at brunch, so don't slap your pregnancy test down next to the pancakes, either!

Newsflash: coffee doesn't count as breakfast

If you're in the midst of trying, or just found out you're already pregnant, you've got to start feeding yourself something besides your usual latte in the morning—no matter how busy, stressed, or totally not hungry you are. The thing is that most of your baby's tiny little vital organs will start to form during the very first weeks of your pregnancy— probably even before you know you're pregnant. And we *both* know you want your son or daughter to be made of stronger stuff than an iced Americano! Also, since your body is working overtime to shift into baby-making mode, you definitely need to be eating enough calories to power you through your day.

The average woman in her twenties or early thirties should consume about 1,800 calories a day, but that number depends on your body mass index (BMI) and how active you are. I know people tend to think that when you're eating for two you need to double up on calories, but experts say you really need to increase your calorie intake only a very little bit—between 100 and 300 extra calories a day! But for now, in the early stages, you *really must* meet the normal 1,800 calories—or whatever the

BMI calorie calculator works out for you—to give your wee one a healthy start. If pre-pregnancy you used to live on salad greens and a handful of M&Ms each day, that's *not* going to cut it anymore. Eating real, balanced meals—meals full of healthy calories that add up to your daily recommended amount based on your BMI (and then more as your pregnancy progresses)—is essential to giving your wee one a chance in this world. Besides, food is delicious!

For everyday eats, your best bets for a quick breakfast are calcium-rich Greek yogurt (many brands have double the protein of regular yogurt!) or even just a bowl of cereal with milk, since calcium will help keep your bones strong while your little one is forming his or her own; orange juice, which has folic acid to help the baby's brain development; or even just a few dried apricots, which are packed with iron, will help keep your energy levels steady, and can be great on top of oatmeal. A little extra nosh in the morning can really help keep you from passing out at that 11 a.m. meeting. Of course, you need more than just breakfast, and there are tons of yummy options to keep you and your baby healthy—so check out the Healthy Eating for Two guide on page 217 for more tips.

So go ahead and indulge yourself once in a while. While pregnancy certainly isn't a time to take up binge eating, it absolutely is a time to be good to yourself and enjoy all the wonderful things your life has to offer. Brunch reservations for you and the girls this weekend? Done and done!

SMART BITS

Of course, in the months to come you're going to gain some weight, but it is important to keep (at least mostly!) to a healthy diet and stay active throughout your pregnancy. The early months are especially important—you're creating healthy eating patterns that will fuel your pregnancy and can extend into your life after delivery. A lot of the extra pounds you'll put on are from the baby itself, and the fluids he or she needs to grow and be protected until the delivery. Recommended weight gain for an average, healthy woman is three to four pounds during the first three months of pregnancy, and then one pound a week after that. If you're ever worried that you're gaining too much weight, just check in with your doc and see what he or she recommends. Baby might not need a midnight peanut-butter-and-jelly sandwich *every* night after all— maybe just once in a while!

Pills to pop—and what to stop

It's awesome that you're starting to eat right, but unless you spend almost all day crunching and munching (which may be tempting), there's almost no way you're going to get all the vitamins and nutrients you need to be your healthiest from food alone. Your doctor might prescribe a certain prenatal vitamin to suit your particular needs, but since not all brands are created equal, here's what to look for when shopping for your prenatal vitamins:

The best prenatal vitamins have . . .

400 mcg folic acid	20 mg niacin
400 IU vitamin D	6 mcg vitamin B12
200–300 mg calcium	10 mg vitamin E
70 mcg vitamin C	15 mg zinc
3 mg thiamin	17 mg iron
2 mg riboflavin	

PAGING DR. GRUNEBAUM

So many vitamins—I swear I'll take them all, but which are the super-important ones and what do they do?

The surgeon general recommends that all women of childbearing age take a vitamin supplement daily. This should specifically include folic acid, which has been found to decrease early pregnancy complications such as miscarriages and also prevent complications such as neural tube defects and heart conditions in the baby.

Optimally, you should be on a vitamin supplement even when not trying to get pregnant, and be on a vitamin supplement at least one to two months before pregnancy begins—but if you haven't taken anything until now, just start!

It is also recommended to take a daily omega-3 supplement. Omega-3 fatty acids are central to pregnancy health and fetal development—they promote neurological growth, and the development of cardiac and circulatory systems—but are not naturally produced by the body, which means you must get them from external food and supplemental sources.

Now, for what to stop? There are a few biggies that you can't afford to ignore at this point.

Ciggies: your baby's biggest enemy

Getting pregnant (and being pregnant!) can be stressful, and I know for so many of you a few puffs are just the thing to calm you down—but cigarettes aren't just bad for *you*, they're absolutely disastrous for your baby. Doctors estimate that 13 percent of fertility problems—that's more than one in 10—are affected by smoking or being around secondhand smoke. Tobacco affects your egg quality, weakens your guy's sperm, and ups your risk for birth defects, miscarriage, and preterm labor. Just not worth it, lady. And quite frankly (and this is where I might get judgy), if you aren't ready to give up smoking, you might not be ready for parenting. When you're a mom you have to put your child first—and the time to start is now.

SMART BITS

People always ask me what I've done in my pregnancies, and for me, the policy is zero tolerance. Zero tolerance for caffeine, except if it's chocolate. Zero tolerance for alcohol, except if it's in a big old hunk of chocolate. And zero tolerance for cigarettes, except for chocolate— and cigarettes are never chocolate! Some people say one glass of wine won't hurt, but to me, it's not worth the risk. Even if there's just a sliver of a *sliver* of a chance that something could go wrong, I would *always* rather have a healthy baby than a glass of Shiraz. No contest!

I just can't imagine how it would feel to have an unhealthy baby and wonder if it was my fault for drinking or smoking. As a parent, it's hard to not feel responsible for everything—which is why I tend to err on the side of safety in every case.

Your daily caffeine IV drip

I'm not going to even try to say you can't have one cup of coffee in the morning (although your doctor might), but some studies have shown that having much more than 200 milligrams of caffeine per day—about one 8-ounce cup of java or two 8-ounce cups of black tea—can cause a miscarriage. Because caffeine crosses the placenta, it can impact the baby's heart rate at any point in your pregnancy and even lead to stillbirth—so definitely don't cheat on this one! Start cutting back little by little, experiment with half regular and half decaf for a while if you need to, and then just stick to your one cup a day. And no extra-grandes!

That said, watch your decaf coffee intake, too. Anything that is normally caffeinated (like coffee or tea) has to go through a chemical process to have the caffeine removed. There are a few different processes that can be used, and which one your coffee or tea company uses matters. Two kinds, "indirect decaffeination" and the "Swiss water process," are both safe, as the coffee or tea that you consume never comes in direct contact with the chemical solvent used to separate the caffeine from the coffee beans or tea leaves. That said, some companies still use a "direct process" in which the beans or leaves come into direct contact with the chemical solvent, meaning they may contain more substantial amounts of these harsh chemicals. So take a second to read packages, and ask baristas what they're pouring into your cup.

PAGING DR. GRUNEBAUM

I've heard so many different studies about alcohol—some even saying a glass of wine during pregnancy is safe. Is that just some wacko fantasy, or is it for real?

I've heard all of these things, too, so let's first get one thing straight: alcohol is a major contributor to fetal and neonatal development problems, potentially leading to fetal alcohol syndrome—both when you are pregnant and when you are trying to get pregnant. There is no known safe amount of alcohol during pregnancy. Since alcohol can be damaging even in the smallest amounts, the only safe amount is zero.

I know firsthand what it's like to go through caffeine withdrawal, but when you have that gorgeous little babe in your arms (and you're finally reunited with your venti double latte), you'll be too happy to even *remember* how hard it was to curb the coffee habit.

What about hair dye?

The jury is still a little bit unsure as to the use of hair dye while you've got a bay-bay on board, because very few studies on actual women have ever been done. That said, a lot of research has been done involving animals and the chemicals in hair dyes, and those indicate that coloring your hair should be totally safe. Only a tiny bit of the dye is ever absorbed by your scalp, and that amount is not thought to be enough to cause problems in your little one.

That said, if you want to be on the safe side (which, as you know, I usually do!), I'd follow these guidelines:

- Avoid procedures involving a lot of scalp contact.

- Consider using temporary color instead of permanent, as the chemicals aren't as harsh.

- Opt for highlights instead of a full color.

No need to have gray days just because the stork is on his way!

Stop avoiding your dentist

I know this sounds like a wacky one, but I'm completely serious. First of all, you want those pearlies to shine in all of your "Hey, I'm pregnant!" Facebook pictures—but more important, healthy oral hygiene, specifically having healthy gums, can both help you get pregnant quicker (recent studies show that it takes women with gum disease longer to conceive) and seriously reduce your risk of complications. The American

Academy of Periodontology has found that women with diseased gums or teeth can be up to *seven* times more likely to deliver a preterm or underweight baby. *Mmmhm.* I can hear you calling the dentist now.

If you're already pregnant when you go, make sure your dentist and the technicians know. It's helpful for them to track the health of your teeth before, during, and after pregnancy, as they're a good indicator of your calcium levels and whether or not you'll be at risk for early-onset osteoporosis, which can lead to bone loss (ouch!), after you deliver.

SMART BITS

Contrary to popular belief, it's absolutely fine to eat sushi and sashimi during pregnancy. There are zero studies that link raw fish to negative health implications for mothers or developing babies—as long as the mother sticks to low-mercury fish like salmon or shrimp. If you stay away from fish like fresh tuna, swordfish, mackerel, shark, and tilefish, all of which have elevated levels of mercury—and eat sushi only at reputable restaurants (no questionable corner takeout for you!)—you can have up to two 6-ounce servings per week. Yum!

I have rights, don't I?
Figuring out maternity leave

I know you're working on having this baby like it's your full-time job, but chances are you've got *another* job—one that pays the bills, provides your insurance, and that you kind of need to think about right now! No, you don't need to tell your boss that you're trying to have a baby, or even let him or her know right away after you find out, but it *is* a good idea to start looking into what kind of maternity leave and benefits—if any— you're entitled to through your employer.

Lots of women assume they're eligible for three months of maternity leave, but so many women actually don't have that available to them. The Family and Medical Leave Act, which is what allows for these 12 weeks of unpaid leave each year to care for your family without jeopardizing your position or your health benefits, applies only to women who work for companies with at least 50 employees at or within 75 miles of their office and who have been at the same company for at least a year, working a minimum of 1,250 hours annually.

State laws vary, and some companies go way above and beyond, offering paid leave or even a longer time off to bond with your wee one. Scan your employer's HR benefits booklet to see what's offered to you, and contact the National Partnership for Women and Families (the people behind the Family and Medical Leave Act) at their website, nationalpartnership.org, if you have any questions.

Hunting for doctors

So, sweetcheeks, I hear you want to give birth in the middle of a field of daisies, with a (medically trained) unicorn prancing nearby and the sound of a babbling brook as your soundtrack. That's wonderful, and I sincerely hope it happens for you, but, um, you might want a backup plan just in case Doc Unicorn bails on you.

Which takes us to picking a doctor. Before starting to look for the right person, though, you need to think about what kind of birth you want for your child. There are basically three options:

• **Hospital birth:** You'll deliver your wee one vaginally, or through C-section if needed, in a hospital setting with doctors, nurses, a full range of pain management interventions available should you want them, and emergency care on hand just in case.

- **Birthing center:** At these home-like centers, you'll deliver your baby vaginally with the assistance of a midwife and nurses—but will have the comfort of knowing there's a doctor on call and a hospital nearby in case of emergency, such as the sudden necessity of a C-section. Some hospitals even house birthing centers, which makes emergency intervention even easier if needed.

- **Home birth:** You will stay at home and give birth vaginally with the aid of a midwife, without medication or any other medical interventions. This is an option only for women at very low risk for complications in pregnancy or delivery. If complications arise, you may need to be transferred to a hospital, which can take time.

Of course this choice is yours to make, but you have to choose the birth plan that takes into account your personal circumstances and is going to be best for your baby and you. This decision should not be self-indulgent in any way. Really weigh what might be best for your child—which is, obviously, the most important factor of all! I know just *thinking* about the big day can make even the toughest of us feel a bit wobbly in the knees, but even though we moms go through a ton, our babies may be going through something even *more* challenging: they're entering the world for the first time, breathing on their own, and feeling air against their fragile little bodies outside the safety of your womb. I know you want to make this experience as safe and trouble-free as possible, so seriously think about the risks involved in each of your options before settling on one.

PAGING DR. GRUNEBAUM

What are your thoughts on giving birth in the hospital versus at home?

It's clearly desirable to have labor and delivery under the most convenient and comfortable circumstances, and there are some women who feel they cannot get that in a hospital and so choose to give birth at home. Out of roughly four million births each year, fewer than 1 percent of American babies are born in private homes. There is no reliable data on how many of these home births result in healthy babies, because people do not have to report what happens in their homes. From the data that exists, however, we do know that of mothers who plan on giving birth at home, roughly 20 percent have to be transferred to a hospital due to complications.

If you are considering a home birth, you need to understand all the facts. Giving birth at home may definitely be more convenient at times, but along with that comfort comes a lack of support available for you and the baby at the hospital including trained pediatricians, experienced obstetricians, and a full nursing staff who can help as needed. If you are leaning toward a home birth because you would rather give birth without pain medications, or because you would like a water birth, it's likely that your local birthing center or hospital can work with you to help make these accommodations in a safer setting.

I know you might think that if you have a low-risk pregnancy, you won't need such specialists on hand, but there is no way of predicting these things. Just the other day at the hospital, we delivered a patient's second baby. It was a low-risk birth, she did not need an episiotomy, the baby was born relatively easily, and the placenta was delivered 10 minutes after the baby was born. Minutes later, though, the woman started to hemorrhage excessively. We had to use everything in our power, including blood transfusion and the knowledge of 12 different doctors and nurses, to save her life. Had this happened at home, the time to bring her to the hospital would not have been sufficient, and that newborn baby would have lost his mother. And it is not only mothers who are at risk at home, but babies as well. American babies who are delivered at home are four times more likely to die than babies born in a hospital. The numbers are still very low in our country, but if it happens, it is always obviously devastating.

I am not meaning to scare you, but only to tell you the facts so you know what kinds of risks you take if you choose to deliver at home. My recommendation is that instead of bringing the delivery room to your home, you try to bring your home and the environment where you want your child to be born into the hospital. You can do this with music, a special pillow, and other things. Talk to your doctor and ask what the hospital will allow in your room. They want to make you comfortable and will be willing to work with you to make the experience as special—and safe—for you as possible.

Once you've figured out your preferred birth strategy, deciding on the right doctor who fits into that plan can be a little daunting. Finding Dr. Grunebaum was obviously an amazing point in my first pregnancy, but it wasn't as if I clicked my ruby-red slippers and magically landed in his office—in fact, the process was pretty difficult. I had a high-risk pregnancy and was rejected by several doctors at first (yes, that can happen!). Dr. Grunebaum happened to be the doctor who was both qualified to handle my potential issues and available to take me on, but believe me, it took us a long time to find each other.

Luckily, Dr. Grunebaum and I also got along, which is a super-important factor in any medical relationship. On paper, a doctor can be perfect—he or she went to the right schools, the office is close to your office, the doctor is old enough to be experienced but not *so* old that he or she doesn't know all the latest medical research. But then in reality? This same doctor may not take the time to listen to you, he or she could be in a practice where you rarely see the doctor at all, or you could be made to wait 40 minutes every time you come in. Not exactly your dream doc.

You might not even want to search for a new doctor if you like your ob-gyn and think that doctor would be a great partner throughout your journey. The important thing is to ask yourself if you feel comfortable with the doctor you're considering. You need someone you can trust completely and who you think will have the time to really dedicate him- or herself to your pregnancy. Here are a few things to consider:

- Is the doctor affiliated with a hospital close to your home?

- Would it be easy to get to routine appointments?

- Does the doctor agree with your birth strategy?

- If you have questions between appointments (and you will!), will the doctor be available to chat with you via email or text?

- Can this doctor commit to delivering your baby, or would the baby be delivered by someone else in his or her practice? Are you okay with that?

- What days does the doctor take appointments (and what days is he or she delivering babies)?

- Does this doctor's practice accept your health insurance?

- If you experience pregnancy or delivery complications, can this doctor stick with you or will you have to transfer to another doctor?

The big thing to remember here is that even if a doctor does meet a lot of your requirements and seems good, you need to *trust* and feel comfortable with this person. If you meet a well-respected doctor and just don't get a good feeling from him or her, move on.

If you're considering going the alternative route with a midwife—as more and more women are—make sure she's certified by the American Midwifery Certification Board, and get at least a couple of references. She should also have a backup plan, should you experience complications through your pregnancy that would make a more traditional medical professional necessary. The best midwives have relationships with doctors and hospitals just in case their clients need that extra help—make sure yours does, too!

SMART BITS

In no way do I want to bring you down from the amazing excitement of trying to get pregnant or finding out you're expecting a little one, which is why I'm going to try to make this bit as quick as possible. There's really no way for me to make it fun or zippy. Having experienced miscarriage and the devastating feelings of loss that go along with that, and knowing other women who've been there too, I knew I'd have to put this rain cloud of a Smart Bit in here somewhere. Just bear with me, because it's helpful for everybody to know.

Miscarriages in the first trimester can certainly happen, but remember they are not what happens most of the time, so there is no need to walk around for your whole first trimester with a sense of fear. That said, Dr. Grunebaum and other experts say roughly 30 to 40 percent of all pregnancies end in miscarriage, so they are important to talk about. Possible miscarriage is also why some of you might not want to wait until you're 12 weeks along to have your first big appointment. I know, it sounds like I've lost my marbles, but hear me out.

It is immensely difficult to describe how hard miscarriage is to deal with. You see, from the moment you find out you are pregnant, even if you are just a few weeks along, you feel completely and utterly 100 percent pregnant. The way you eat, the way you think, the way you look at the world changes. All of a sudden your whole world is different, even if you haven't announced it to everyone yet. You are a *mother*.

So if you should experience a loss, and find out even as early as 12 weeks, it can be devastating. In my case, the only thinking that got me through was knowing that my fertilized egg just wasn't healthy enough to support a thriving, happy baby. And if I was going to have another child (which I eventually did!), I wanted it to have the most solid foundations for life possible. When you finally get to hold your baby in your arms—no matter how he or she gets there—you know that whatever you went through to get there was all worthwhile.

The first trimester can be an anxiety-ridden time—many women are very fearful of going through a miscarriage, or indeed may have had one already and fear another. These first few weeks can be nerve-wracking, *especially* when the general practice is for women to wait until around the 12-week mark to have their first obstetrics appointment and finally get that much-needed sigh of relief that all looks good. Having been in that very situation myself, I recently learned a wonderful thing: it's absolutely possible to get an appointment at *eight* weeks instead of 12. You can find out a month earlier how things are really going. A healthy heartbeat and ultrasound at eight weeks indicates that the miscarriage rate has dropped to less than 10 percent, compared to less than 5 percent at 12 weeks.

I know I would have loved being able to breathe a little easier during my second pregnancy—having a whole extra month with this information rather than living with anxiety until the 12th week. And quite honestly, I believe the less stressed you are, the better environment your body is for your baby.

If you're feeling overwhelmed and have reason to be worried (such as a previous miscarriage, or if you've had problems conceiving—or you are simply just a little nervous), request an earlier appointment! If your doctor's office resists when you call to tell them that you are pregnant and want to schedule your first appointment, explain *why* you are anxious. I know it can be strange sharing these things with a stranger, but trust me when I say that the receptionists at ob-gyns' offices have heard *everything*. If they aren't sensitive to your concerns, then perhaps you need to consider finding a new doctor, or asking to speak to your doctor directly.

What's a tribe?

Trust me, I know you're organized, on top of things, and generally the queen of your castle with everything in control (or you're expert at making it look that way!), but even the strongest women among us need a little help here and there as we become mommies. In my mother's generation, and grandmother's before that, families stayed closer together geographically, providing an at-your-fingertips "tribe" of support for new moms. Not only is that not the case now, but today our moms are often more likely to give us career advice than to guide us through Baby 101! This generation of educated "glamour nanas" is amazing for other reasons, though. They're way more active than the generation before them (they can really keep up with the little ones when they come to visit!), and a lot of them know what it's like to be working mothers—a talent that doesn't come easily to many of us.

While we have a lot more medical knowledge available than previous generations, and wonderful new inventions that can make parenting easier (hello, magical diaper pail!), today it's up to us to build our own "tribe" of people who can support us through pregnancy and early motherhood. It's not that we've lost our female mothering instinct, or that we need more help than other generations did, it's just that societies have shifted in a way that means we have to seek out and piece together tribes for ourselves. Our mothers can and should almost always be a part of that tribe, but we need some other people, too.

Throughout this book, chapter by chapter, I'll help you add the right people to your tribe, and help you get the most from this awesome group of people who adore you, and your babe-to-be, to bits. It's going to be an incredible journey, and you'll be so happy to have your tribe by your side from start to finish and beyond.

Who's in your tribe now?

- ○ Your partner and/or your best friend
- ○ Your doctor or midwife

A note on partners

In today's world, one of the most beautiful things is that families are all so different. We list partners in your tribe, and throughout the book, because we believe it's wonderful to have someone who's right there with you, as a partner, for this amazing journey. It can be your husband, your boyfriend, your girlfriend, your mother, a sister, your pastor or rabbi—basically anyone but your dog! As long as that person is your go-to support, he or she fits the bill. And in the case that you don't have anyone and you're truly going this alone, let *me* be your partner through this. Right now is your time, and you're building a brand-new family all of your own. It's an honor to be on the ride with you.

Murmurs from the Man Cave

Welcome to the Man Cave, where dads get honest and share their thoughts on their partners' bodies, their relationships, and their babies-to-be. I've talked with over 100 recent real-life dads and asked them to describe what each stage of their wife or girlfriend's pregnancy was *really* like for them. So many men, my husband included, don't know how to articulate what they're experiencing (or are afraid of being put in the doghouse for telling their wives or girlfriends how they're really feeling!), but *not* hearing from your partner can cause misunderstandings and hurt, and ultimately weaken relationships.

For this reason, I'm excited to bring you into the Man Cave, a space at the end of each chapter where I'll share—anonymously, we don't want anybody getting in trouble—highlights of what my guy panel told me. Sometimes funny, sometimes thoughtful, always revealing, input from the Man Cave will open your eyes to just how excited, anxious, worried, or just plain confused guys can be throughout this journey, and help you strengthen your relationship before the baby even gets here.

Keep in mind that although your partner is probably too smart to say some of these things to you directly (he doesn't want to sleep on the couch, after all!), he very well may be thinking them and deserves some compassion. You're a team—and you'll be an even better one for your baby if you communicate and make the extra effort to understand each other through this final stretch. And now, on to the first big question!

What went through your head when you first learned you were expecting a baby?

"Holy sh*t! We did it!"

"Surprise! We had stopped trying, so I wasn't expecting it. I realized in that moment that this was going to change our lives forever."

"With my first two, I was just really worried about how we were going to make it on a single income."

"#%$@#^&, I thought I would get at least *one* year of marriage before pregnancy. I've been tricked. I'm not ready for this, and neither is my marriage."

"I was totally blown away. We're talking so floored that I had to pull my truck over—I was on the road when I heard the news!"

The takeaway

Learning that you're going to be a parent is such a huge, life-changing moment, whether you were expecting it or not. It's easy to get caught up in all the changes your body will be going through, but remember to take time, both while you're trying to conceive and once you've finally got that positive test in your hands, to really talk with your partner about what a baby will mean to your relationship and your lifestyle—and for heaven's sake, let him know about any insecurities *you're* feeling. Your partner might be worried, upset, nervous, or totally dumbstruck, but that's normal and natural when you're faced with something as huge as a new baby. Asking about, and listening to, how your partner's feeling will help him feel more connected and supported throughout this incredible adventure.

Months Two and Three

finally feeling pregnant

Mommy IQ:
What you'll be figuring out this month

○ Baby's achievements

○ Hey, Doc! What's baby's sign?

○ Telling your parents you had sex—and it worked

○ Keeping baby under wraps (for now)

○ Morning sickness: not just for mornings anymore

○ Sex (when the baby's in there)

○ Who's in your tribe?

○ Murmurs from the Man Cave

{ My **Mommy IQ** is ___ out of 8 }

One of the things that people find so shocking about pregnancy is the sheer exhaustion. For something so tiny, that growing baby just takes everything out of you and consumes your thoughts day in and day out. With every child I've had, from the very first day I learned I was pregnant my brain went completely off-the-wall berserk. I run out and buy the biggest sandwich I can find because, *hello*, I need to feed this baby! Then I complain about how tight my pants suddenly are (probably from the foot-long sandwich I've just eaten, but *of course* I think it's because of the baby), and then I proceed to sleep for about 14 hours to rest up for delivery—which is months and months away.

When I wake up, I realize I need to get back to reality, get back to work, and be a person again—but my "pregnant brain" continues to kick in throughout the whole nine plus months and doesn't disappear until my little babe is in my arms. So, if you're feeling a little distracted, give yourself a break (even though Dr. G swears there's no scientific evidence of pregnancy affecting your brain!). Your mind, your body, your . . . *everything* . . . isn't ever going to be quite the same again. Embrace it! You are about to become something more wonderful than you can even imagine—a mother.

Rosie's maternity mantras

You are officially on your way, and so many awesome and unbelievable moments are ahead of you. You might be tired right now, you might feel rather vomitacious*, but trust me that every minute of this is worth it. The good news? After a few weeks, you'll likely be feeling so much better and really be able to celebrate this happy time (as you should!). If you're just joining in now and haven't read the first chapter since you already know you're pregnant, go back and read it anyway. There's tons of good stuff in there to help you get your ducks in a row. And whether or not you're already up to speed (I know, so much information can be overwhelming!), here are a couple of thoughts to get you through the hard times.

> * Rosie, Decoded
> **Vomitacious (*adj.*):** The opposite of delicious, usually followed by a quick but unmistakable gagging sound. A word you might be using frequently right about now.

> " What lies behind us and what lies before us are tiny matters compared to **what lies within us.**"
>
> —HENRY S. HASKINS, AUTHOR

> " I don't know why they call it 'morning sickness' when it's **all f#@!ing day long.** Unless it's M-O-U-R-N, as in 'mourning the loss of your single life.' "
>
> —MIRANDA HOBBES, *SEX AND THE CITY*

Baby's achievements

It might not seem like much is going on in there, since you can't feel your little one moving around yet and you're likely barely showing (if at all!), but I promise, your babe is already a teeny tiny wonder.

At week eight, your baby will be roughly the size of your thumbnail, and by the end of week 12, he or she will be as big as your favorite nail polish bottle—and have the beginnings of his or her own fingernails and toenails! Color me impressed.

Someone's preparing for a sense-ational future—during these early weeks, your little honey is forming eye lenses, ear indentations, tiny nostrils, and a mouth perforation. Think about it: All of the beautiful and exciting things your baby will hear, see, smell, and say over the course of his or her lifetime have their roots in you, right now. It's kind of overwhelming to imagine, but mainly it's just incredible—and it should make giving up all those bad habits and taking care of yourself a piece of cake. After all, it's not just about you anymore.

By the end of month three, boys will be boys and girls will be girls. That's right—your little one's Queen Victoria* or Prince Albert* has started to form. It's still too tiny for your doctor to tell you for sure whether you're going to have a son or a daughter, but if the anticipation is killing you (I'm always beyond impatient to know), rest assured that you'll be able to find out soon.

* Rosie, Decoded

Queen Victoria (*noun, singular*): My own ladylike way of referring to the down-there lady bits. And come on, admit it—yours deserves a tiara.

Prince Albert (*noun, singular*): My preferred term for his down-there bits. Hearing myself say any of the more traditional terms for it makes me cringe or laugh! I know, I know. I'm a child!

Hey, Doc!
What's baby's sign?

It's time for your 12-week prenatal checkup. Every time I go to the doctor when I'm pregnant, I'm freaked out and want to see the baby's heartbeat—but there's absolutely nothing like being at that first 12-week appointment and realizing that even though you're not showing, there's really a baby in there who's moving around and thriving. It's very emotional. It's like, finally! I'm *really* pregnant! There's a bay-bay inside of me! As you know from the last chapter, though, I've also been on the other side of it where I've gotten the most disappointing news. I know just how much anxiety, hope, and even fear can be built up into this day. So, take a deep breath and get that examination gown on. No matter what, you're going to get through this—hopefully with a new little bundle of love in tow!

Some of you might be seeing two or more little heartbeats, which means—congrats multiplied—you're having multiples! While having more than one baby in a pregnancy can be a blessing, it also means you will need to keep a few things in mind. Don't panic, but do try to be as informed as possible about any possible complications or difficulties you and your babies might encounter. For more on multiples, see pages 239–41 in the Tricky Bits section.

Among so many other things, your 12-week appointment is the day when your doctor will tell you when your happiest day—the day when you finally get to meet your gorgeous new baby—might happen. To determine that, your doctor will need to know the approximate date of the first day of your last period, so try to come prepared with that date handy. Your due date is 40 weeks after that date (which is actually closer to 10 months as we count them than nine). It's important to realize, though, that your approximate due date may change when your doctor sees the baby's growth through ultrasounds, and that very few babies come exactly when they were predicted to arrive! Make sure to bring someone with you—your partner, a good friend, or your mom—are always good bets. You'll also want a notepad to scribble down the billions of things your doctor will likely recommend.

Your doctor will want to run a bunch of tests and go over a lot of information with you, so make sure you give yourself two to three hours there, just in case. Besides a blood test to check your basic health, you'll be getting a standard pelvic exam with a Pap test—just the same as you get at your annual lady appointment, but this time you'll be more likely to bleed or spot a bit afterward, as your cervix has softened a little since you got pregnant and is slightly more sensitive. If you see a little red in the days following your appointment, don't freak—the baby isn't at risk.

That's the basic overview, but for the nitty-gritty what-the-hell-are-they-actually-doing-to-me details, I went to Dr. Grunebaum for the inside scoop. Check this chart to see what your doctor is testing for, what the procedure will be like (lots of these can be read in just one blood test), and why each test is important.

test	why it's done	how it's done
complete blood count (cbc)	checks for anemia, blood diseases, platelet count	**blood test**
rh factor	a mother's negative rh factor may be a problem if she develops antibodies against the baby's red cells	**blood test**
antibody (coombs test)	certain antibodies, such as kell, can harm the fetus	**blood test**
hemoglobin electrophoresis	tests for abnormal hemoglobins (e.g., sickle cell, thalassemia)	**blood test**
hepatitis b antigen	if there is hb antigen present, the baby can become infected at birth	**blood test**

test	why it's done	how it's done
syphilis screen	syphilis can be treated with antibiotics to prevent fetal and newborn infection	**blood test**
hiv screen	hiv can be treated in pregnancy to prevent the baby from becoming infected	**blood test**
rubella (german measles)	a positive test shows that the mother is immune	**blood test**
varicella (chickenpox) antibody	a positive test shows immunity	**blood test**
genetic screen	testing for cystic fibrosis is done routinely. other tests are done for patients in certain ethnic groups	**blood test**

test	why it's done	how it's done
rubeola (measles) antibody	a positive test shows immunity	**blood test**
parvovirus antibody (optional)	a positive test shows immunity	**blood test**
toxoplasma antibody (optional)	a positive test shows immunity	**blood test**
cytomegalovirus antibody (optional)	a positive test shows partial immunity	**blood test**
urine test for protein, ketones, leucocytes, urine culture	treatment is indicated if tests are abnormal	**urine analysis**
pap (papanicolaou) cervix smear	an abnormal pap smear result needs to be further evaluated	**pelvic exam**
cervix screen for gonorrhea and chlamydia	both infections can be treated with antibiotics	**pelvic exam**
tuberculosis (ppd) screen (if at risk)	treatment is important if necessary	**skin test**

SMART BITS

For most people, the 12-week appointment marks the end of anxiety, but for some it can be the beginning of more. If you choose to have the nuchal fold scan, which is recommended, it will be performed around this time. Between your blood tests and some measurements on the ultrasound, your doctor will be able to tell you the probability of your baby having chromosomal abnormalities that cause conditions such as Down syndrome. Your nuchal fold scan results will come back in about a week, and will tell you the likelihood of an abnormality. This percentage either falls within normal range for your age, so you don't need to worry, or falls outside that range—a result that can be alarming. If you are in the latter category (which I have been before, so I know just how it feels), you will almost certainly be sent to a genetic counselor to discuss the results. From there you will have to make some hard decisions. It's a confusing time, so please don't hesitate to ask your doctor questions. You chose your doctor for a reason—you trust him or her—and now is the time to lean on that person's expertise more than ever.

False positives are not uncommon, so that may be what is going on if you receive an abnormal result. The problem with the nuchal fold scan, though, is that it's impossible to know *for sure* whether there is in fact a problem unless you do further, more invasive testing, such as chorionic villus sampling (CVS), which would happen before 13 weeks, or amniocentesis between 16 and 18 weeks. These tests come with their own risks. Though fewer than 1 percent of CVS tests lead to miscarriage, still, some do—so you have to weigh your need to know against the risk of the test.

When my nuchal results came back, I was told that my baby had a one-in-99 chance of a chromosomal abnormality. My husband and I were of course worried, and decided to have the CVS done so we could prepare if in fact the abnormality existed for us. In the end, we turned out *not* to be that one in 99.

The decision of whether to do the nuchal scan, and then whether to follow up with further testing, is a deeply personal one, and I can't make that call for you. Listen to your doctor and your genetics counselor and decide what is best for your family in your particular situation. Every situation is different, every family is different, and these moments—no matter how hard they are, and I know firsthand that they're very hard—are the ones that are preparing you to know what's best for your child in the long run.

The fun part of this appointment, though (after all that, you deserve some fun!), is the ultrasound—when, for the very first time, you get to see your tiny miracle snuggled up inside you. Even with my third child, seeing her there inside me, knowing she was real, not just someone I'd dreamed up, was unlike anything else I've ever experienced. Your baby isn't big enough yet for the doc to get a clear view of whether you're having a boy or a girl, but just seeing his or her tiny arms and legs and head and nose is magic enough.

PAGING DR. GRUNEBAUM

Tell me about the nuchal fold scan. I'm not sure if I'll have one or not, but I want to know about it.

The nuchal fold scan, where the back of the neck of the fetus is measured, together with a blood test, can help determine the risk of genetic abnormalities such as Down syndrome and others. Research has shown this test can also indicate other anomalies such as heart problems. No one has to have this test done, but I think it's a good idea, as it can help prepare you and your family for any challenges that may arise further into your pregnancy or after your child is born.

That said, if your doctor says the risks are increased that your baby may have an abnormality, there is no way to know what's really going on for sure unless you have further testing. You may be referred to a specialist, such as a genetic counselor, who can tell you about all of your options, including further testing that you may choose to have done. For more information on genetic abnormalities and these tests, please refer to the Tricky Bits section on pages 238–39, where I go into greater detail.

Telling your parents you had sex— and it worked

Some people blab with their moms about sexy time as if they were discussing the six o'clock news, but let's just say, I'm *not* that kind of girl! The thought of even watching a Hollywood love scene with my parents makes me all squirmy—so you can imagine how I would feel talking about my own baum-chicka-baum-baum adventures at family dinner. And you know what? That's essentially what you're doing when you tell your family about your pregnancy. To be honest, I'm not exactly sure who the "I'm pregnant" talk was more awkward for—me or them—but then I'm English and probably sexually repressed, so, um, just ignore my crazytunes squeamishness!

The good news is that your parents will be too thrilled about their future grandchild to think about you and your guy in compromising positions. The tricky news is that they might be *so* thrilled about their coming grandchild that they try to dictate exactly how you should plan your pregnancy, how you should plan for the baby, and exactly what kind of parents you should be. And all of those things that they'll dictate are probably exactly what they did with you—which is what most of us would like to avoid!

Be prepared for this, and try, try, *try* not to lose it and get angry. Your parents and in-laws love you and are just trying to help you in the way they know how—and the way they know how is what they did. I mean, they must have done some things right— you and your partner are still standing, after all! That said, don't let family trample all over this amazing time in your life. Set the ground rules and set them early. If they recommend doing something you're not into, just thank them for their advice, and tell them it's so helpful to have as much information as possible from your loved ones and your doctor—because it will all help *you* make the best decisions for *your* journey. Believe me, taking this road is far less painful than telling your mother that you absolutely will not be following her advice. And besides? No matter how crazytown she might sound right now, she's one of the most important members of your tribe, and she—and your dad and your in-laws—probably have a ton of really useful tips and tricks up their sleeves that you'll be thankful for down the road. They have, after all, been here before!

Keeping baby under wraps (for now)

Just because you want your mom and dad to share in your joy doesn't mean it's time to go *totally* public with your news. Most people wait until between weeks eight and 12 to spread the news beyond their immediate families, but not everybody is good at keeping such an exciting secret. It's really *your* decision about whom to tell and when—but a rule of thumb I think is smart to follow, at least in the first eight weeks of pregnancy, is to tell only those people you'd be comfortable telling about a miscarriage. We all hope that won't happen, but it's a reality and until the risk goes down, you might not want to shout your mommy-to-be status from the rooftops.

On the flip side, don't be pressured to *not* celebrate if you really want to scream your happy news from the rooftops. Every woman has her own motivations and her own comfort level. Do what you want, but know why you're doing it. Here are a few tricks I've learned over the years to keep my pregnancy news quiet until I'm ready to tell the world:

- Wear empire-waist tops with leggings and swingy jackets—those pieces are great for hiding the little extra-sumthin-sumthin you're carrying, but won't scream "I'm preeeeegnaaant!" in the way that a baby-doll dress might (save those for later!).

- Make sure your parents and in-laws know they don't have the green light to post the happy news online, and that they should refrain from putting that "proud grandparent" bumper sticker on their car until you're ready to make the big reveal.

- If you have to leave during the workday for a prenatal checkup, just tell your boss you have a doctor's appointment—it's none of her business what kind of doctor you're seeing, and you don't have to tell her even if she asks.

- When you're at dinner with friends, go ahead and order a drink—in fact, order something over-the-top that you don't even like so you're not tempted to take a sip. Then, once everybody else is knee-deep in their own margaritas, Manhattans, and mimosas, they'll never even notice when you don't drink yours. And if someone does say something? Just tell them your stomach's been a bit iffy lately (probably true anyway!) and you're sadly going to have to skip this one.

Morning sickness: not just for mornings anymore

If you feel like you're going throw up first thing in the morning, and before breakfast, and after breakfast, and before lunch, and after lunch, and before dinner, and well, *all the time*—congratulations, you're pregnant! There are many different degrees and differences in the ways mommies-to-be feel sick when they're newly pregnant. Some women don't feel sick much at all; some women feel pretty rotten all day for a while. I wish I had some magical cure for you, but the truth is there's no way to skip morning sickness (or, rather, just *sickness*) entirely. That said, there *are* ways of curbing it so you can go on with your life.

Some experts recommend eating small, frequent meals, but if you're on the go as much as I am, you probably don't have time to sit down for a small plate every three to four hours. Since the trick is never letting yourself get too hungry, I've found carrying simple snacks like dried fruit, a little bag of almonds, sour gummy candies, or even a few plain crackers in my bag to munch on between mealtimes helps keep the biggest nausea waves at bay. Also, consider ginger your new BFF—ginger tea, ginger ale, and even ginger candies can help calm your tummy so you can stay on track.

The name of the game is to never be caught anywhere without a snack. You know how moms always have snacks in their bag for their kids? Well, that needs to start right now.

PAGING DR. GRUNEBAUM

Almonds? Really? Is it safe to eat nuts at this stage in my pregnancy? I've heard something about how my baby might have a nut allergy if I do.

Almonds, really! Unless you yourself have a sensitivity to nuts, you can absolutely eat nuts throughout your pregnancy. They're a terrific source of protein and other nutrients your baby needs. There's no data that says otherwise.

I know that when you feel sick, sometimes the last thing you want to do is put anything else in your stomach, but the truth is that eating is often the only thing that's actually going to keep you from feeling sick or even vomiting. Some people think they just can't keep anything down, but try anyway, and make sure to drink tons of water and stay hydrated. Getting dehydrated will only make you feel so much sicker, so drink up, lady!

Oh, and keep a pack of mints in your purse, too. Even with a full arsenal of weapons to ward off morning sickness, you *will* lose the battle once in a while, and it's amazing how a quick burst of mint can keep you from feeling completely defeated.

PAGING DR. GRUNEBAUM

So, Dr. G, I get it that even though morning sickness is awful, it's worth it to have that super-sweet babe in your arms—but why does it happen? Is it helping the baby somehow?

Morning sickness is caused by a rise in the human chorionic gonadotropin (hCG) pregnancy hormone that occurs with pregnancy shortly after implantation. This hormone is necessary in the formation of the placenta, which will nourish the fetus as it grows and becomes a real baby—so yes, there is a reason for it! Symptoms of pregnancy and morning sickness can occur when your hCG reaches a certain level, usually shortly after you miss your period. It is completely normal and occurs in 70 to 80 percent of all pregnancies.

Morning sickness usually disappears with the normal drop of the hCG pregnancy hormone, around the 10th to 12th week. Some women experience morning sickness throughout their entire pregnancy, and some may never experience it at all. It does not harm your baby, unless the sickness becomes so severe that you are unable to hold down food enough to keep nutrients in your body to allow the baby to grow. If you're experiencing extreme vomiting or other symptoms, definitely let your doctor know. It's very rare, but you could need extra medical care.

What if I'm actually sick and not just morning sick? What kind of over-the-counter medications can I take to feel better?

Of course you want to see your doctor if you're not feeling well, as any illness could be a sign of something more going on with your baby that needs attention.

My first recommendation is to get back to basics and make yourself (or get someone else to make you) a nice pot of chicken noodle soup. It's comforting, and the nutrients will help your body fight off a random cold or bug that is bothering you.

That said, if you feel you must take something, acetaminophen, or Tylenol, is absolutely safe for both you and your baby—even in the "extra strength" formula. Do not hesitate to take it if it will give you some relief, but of course follow the instructions on the package and do not take more than directed.

Aspirin should not be taken unless your doctor specifically recommends otherwise—which he or she might in certain situations. Taking aspirin during pregnancy has been linked to miscarriage, slower growth of the fetus, and delayed labor, so please do not take this unless you are doing so under the care of your doctor.

Excedrin can contain both aspirin and caffeine, neither of which is recommended during pregnancy.

Ibuprofen, or Advil, also is not recommended during this time, as it has been linked with birth defects when taken early in pregnancy; it is absolutely off-limits during the third trimester, when it can lead to lung or heart damage in your baby.

Stick with Tylenol, and if that isn't working for you, ask your doctor for advice on what else can be done.

Sex (when the baby's in there)

Trust me when I tell you that it makes me uncomfortable to talk not just about sex, but about *how* you should be having sex—yet I feel it's my duty to relay all important information to you. And having sex? Um, *hello,* important!

First off, your baby isn't going to be hurt (or psychologically traumatized!) by a little hanky-panky—but your *relationship* could be if you don't find time for a bedtime romp now and then. Your hormones have seriously started to run amuck, meaning that your libido could either be raging or completely asleep—but either way, you need to nurture your relationship just like you're nurturing your baby, and one of the best ways of doing that is by making sure your bedroom sees more action than your nightly snoring.

I'm going to do a little "wham-bam-thank-you-ma'am" here with my tips. No need to go into any uncomfortable details—you know what to do between the sheets!—but it is important for you to know these few things:

- Pretty much any position that feels good to you is fine—but you might find that it's uncomfortable to lie flat on your back, especially once you reach the third trimester and the weight of your baby is too much for your organs to handle in that position. Plus, lying on your back can decrease blood flow to the uterus, placenta, and baby—not what you want. Cowgirl, anyone? Yeehaw!

- Oral sex is fine (and fun!), but it's incredibly important that your partner doesn't blow any air up your vaginal canal. It's rare, but a burst of air up there right now could actually put your life—and your baby's—at risk. It's also good to note that since you're likely dealing with a bit of nausea, this might not be the best time to, ahem, taste what Prince Albert has to offer.

- If your partner is going in the back door, don't let him back in the front without either changing the condom, if he's using one, or washing up. Same rule applies to toys.

- If you are using toys, opt for silicone-based toys that can be boiled after use to kill any bacteria that might have gotten on them. Now is not the time to invite any suspect germs to meet your Queen Victoria. And silicone-based or not, it's *always* a good idea to pop a fresh condom on a toy before using it. One more sterile barrier never hurts.

Just be creative, go slow, and find something that feels good for both of you. I'm going to zip it at that because *you* know what to do, and besides, this topic is making me blush so much I look like a stoplight!

Who's in your tribe?

You've already got:

○ Your partner and/or your best friend

○ Your doctor or midwife

And you're adding:

○ Your parents and in-laws

Murmurs from the Man Cave

Welcome back to the Man Cave! This month, our guys are feeling a little frisky and the conversation has turned to the place where the magic happens, ladies. That's right—their minds (as they often are!) are focused squarely on the bedroom. Let's listen in on what pregnancy's got to do with it.

How did you feel about having sex once you knew there was a baby in there?

"It didn't bother me! Well, at least it didn't after the ob-gyn assured me the baby wouldn't feel anything."

"My wife's sexual appetite was insatiable during each pregnancy, which was unexpected considering how pregnant women are portrayed on television. It was a pleasant surprise."

"There was some frustration because the frequency went down. It's not like my wife didn't want sex at all—I always just figured she totally had the desire, so her mind was still saying Y-E-S, but her body was saying no. Or, you know, I assume that's what a woman feels. Meanwhile our bodies as men are always saying yes! It's all worth it to have a baby, though."

"In the beginning it was fine, but about a month before the baby was due, the doctor told my wife he could feel the baby's head. I was scared that my penis would damage my son's head! I thought if the

doctor could feel it with his hand, I'd be able to hit it.
A week passed without sex till my wife reassured me
all would be well."

The takeaway

First of all, make sure he knows he's not going to bump into the baby (men always think they're larger than they really are, but he's not going all the way to your uterus!). Then keep his ego alive by making sure he knows you're still attracted to him, even if your body isn't exactly up to fulfilling his every fantasy. And really, *never* put sex completely to the side unless your doctor says you have to for medical reasons. What works for you in the bedroom will change as your pregnancy progresses, but using creativity to find out what does work along the way can actually be a big turn-on for both of you.

Month Four
bigger, better baby bumps

Mommy IQ:

What you'll be figuring out this month

○ Baby's achievements

○ Skipping the Olympic trials, but staying fit

○ Prepping your closet to handle some new curves

○ The great childcare search begins

○ It's not ebola, you're just pregnant

○ Who's in your tribe?

○ Murmurs from the Man Cave

{ My **Mommy IQ** is ___ out of 7 }

When I was pregnant with my first child, everyone kept telling me to start looking into childcare immediately, but I was like, "Why?" I mean, maybe other people don't love their babies as much as I was going to love mine, but me and *my* little babe? I knew we'd be inseparable, like a kangaroo mom and her joey. Why would I want him to be with someone else all day when I could just strap him to my chest and take him to the office with me?! I'd get extra bonding in and *he'd* learn how to run a business before first grade—I honestly couldn't understand why all mothers didn't do this. The music from his crib mobile would become background music for conference calls, we'd fly together to LA for meetings (of course he'd have a sharp little suit for those), we'd take power lunches together, and obviously take over the corporate world. Crazy people didn't know what they were talking about!

When my son finally was born, I actually tried my ambitious kangaroo-mom plan for about . . . a day, or until I learned the hard truth. My baby didn't *want* to be schlepped all over town with me—plus, he needed so much attention and affection that I couldn't keep up with my work with him there. I had to scramble to find a nanny at the last minute—and trust me, you don't want to be in that situation! This month I'll walk you through what I should have done near the middle of my pregnancy in terms of childcare, as well as lots of other stuff you can't afford to miss. Get ready for your Mommy IQ to skyrocket!

Rosie's maternity mantras

Holy moly, that little one is growing up a storm and *you*, my lovely, are likely starting to show! As your tummy expands, your clothes stop fitting, and the scale starts saying that you weigh, you weigh . . . "how much?!," you might need a little time to adjust. Just remember that this is all preparing you to be an incredible mommy to your little one! None of these changes are happening as punishment for getting pregnant—they're happening because your baby needs them to happen in order to grow and thrive. And as that little one's mother, you obviously want to give him or her everything needed for an amazing start. This whole process is preparing you to be more selfless than you've ever been before—so if you need a little teeny bit of "selfish" time this month—say a whole night of takeout nosh and reality TV—go for it, lady. You've earned it. And as always, I've got a couple of deep thoughts to keep you going this month:

" A ship under sail and a big-bellied woman are the **handsomest** two things that can be seen."

—BENJAMIN FRANKLIN, AMERICAN STATESMAN, INVENTOR, AND DIPLOMAT

" After the first trimester and morning sickness [pregnancy] is **no big thing** . . . except there *is* one big thing—and that's **my bottom!**"

—JENNIFER GARNER, ACTRESS

Baby's achievements

That growth spurt you've been waiting for has finally started—*hello,* belly!—and although you might not be feeling much in the way of the baby's movement now, those kicks are fast approaching. At this point, some women feel a very light fluttering here and there, and some feel almost nothing at all—was that a little gas bubble from the sparkling water you had at lunch or your baby-to-be? It's very different for everybody during these weeks, so try not to obsess!

At this point, your baby is about the size of a pocket camera, and your wee one's brain is starting to develop in a more advanced way. Future valedictorian? Without a doubt.

All that calcium you've been downing has helped transform your angel's bones from rubbery cartilage into a solid structure—and near the end of this month or the start of the next, you will begin to feel him or her testing out brand-new joints with a few kicks and stretches. Whether it's karate or ballet, your little one's starting training early!

By the end of the month, your baby will be coated in a thick white substance called vernix caseosa that protects the skin from the amniotic fluid surrounding him or her. Think of it as a luxurious, beyond-spa-quality moisture wrap for your little one.

Skipping the Olympic trials, but staying fit

I know firsthand just how bonkers you might be going with your new weight, your new body shape, and your new lack of anything that might even vaguely fit you in the closet! It's so tempting to try to knock yourself out with fat-busting workouts right now, but take it from me, being knocked out just isn't worth it.

I learned my lesson the hard way, and hopefully you can just learn it from me. When I was pregnant with my first son, I had the most bodacious bump ever. My stomach was massive, and I was determined to not gain more weight than necessary. One morning, my husband—who'd just finished competing in a triathlon—announced he was going for a run, and I decided to join him, saying I'd just power walk and we'd meet at the end. We walked to the park together and I kissed him goodbye, but then, when I saw him sprint off ahead of me, this crazy competitiveness took over my brain. I thought I must look super lazy to all these svelte gym bunnies running in the park! Gisele says she did kickboxing up until the very end of her pregnancy—*surely* I could do more than power walk. I cranked up the club tunes on my iPod, and the thumpa-thumpa-thumpa beats somehow made me feel like Rocky (if Rocky was about seven months pregnant!). I started hustling down some stairs at a rather ambitious sprint . . . and the next thing I knew, there I was, face-planted on the cement in head-to-toe spandex workout gear, looking not only like an idiot, but like someone who wasn't being careful enough with herself or her baby.

I know why I did it—I was desperate to feel those endorphins that come with a good workout, that feeling that your body can do anything, that you're faster and healthier and better-looking than everyone else. Plus, I hated anyone thinking I was a slacker—especially, for some cuckoo reason, those perfect strangers in the park. But you know what? They could *see* that I was pregnant! They knew—even if I, the totally crazy woman, didn't—that I wasn't exactly up to running marathons (especially since I'd never been much of a runner to start with!). My point in telling you all of this is that although workouts *are* good for you, and you *should* keep moving during your pregnancy, it's also easy to get a little bonkers and overdo it.

That's why I've asked my friend and MomPrep fitness guru extraordinaire Andrea Orbeck to let you in on the tried-and-true pregnancy workout secrets she shares with her top clients. And her top clients aren't anything to sneeze at. You know Heidi Klum, that gorgeous, willowy woman who can pop out a baby and then appear on the Victoria's Secret catwalk—in not much more than a few strings and giant angel wings—literally *weeks* later? Well, it's Andrea who not only keeps Heidi healthy and in amazing shape while she's pregnant so she can make a fast recovery, but also helps her get her pre-baby body back after delivery. And don't think she's one of those get-skinny-at-any-cost trainers, either. Andrea's the real deal—she studied kinesiology at the University of Calgary, is recognized as a pregnancy fitness specialist, and is certified in intracellular physiology, postural assessment, and myofascial release therapy. Phew!

Long story short, Andrea knows what she's talking about and loves helping pregnant women stay healthy, feel great, and look even better. You might not be able to stick to her program every day, and you might still laze in front of the TV with a few cookies now and then, but trust me when I say her advice is the best out there. Listen to her, and do the best you can. I wish I'd had her on hand for my first pregnancy, and now that I've got her, I want to share her wisdom with you. Take it away, Andrea!

Working it out with Andrea

Hey there! I'm thrilled that Rosie asked me to jump in here and help you stay your healthiest during these 10 months leading up to motherhood. There are so many myths and misconceptions out there about fitness during pregnancy, and I want to make sure you know the facts so you can be at your best for the *ultimate marathon*—childbirth!

The thing is, a lot of women only want to work out during pregnancy because they're worried about excess weight gain and they want to look their best—but really, looking good is just a *side effect* of exercise (sure, a *great* side effect, but it isn't the main event). The real benefits are even more amazing. Did you know that when you do cardiovascular exercise—like running, biking, aerobics, or anything that gets your heart pumping—your body is actually able to deliver more oxygen and nutrients to your baby's placenta? There's scientific data that proves it! Plus, keeping active—or getting active—can help ward off gestational diabetes and help manage it if you've already got it. If you want to know more about gestational diabetes, go to page 88.

The important thing to keep in mind is that the intensity of your workout for the next few months really does depend on how active you were for the year or year and a half leading up to your pregnancy. But it also depends on what your doctor advises. I don't know what complications or special concerns you might be facing, but your doc *does*— definitely consult him or her first and get the okay for exercise before following any of my tips. This is one instance (among many!) in which your doctor really does know best!

If the gym is your second home . . .

Let's say you typically run about three days a week, do an express spin class at lunch, and take yoga with the girls on Sunday mornings. (*Phew!*) You probably came into this pregnancy in *amazing* shape— and unless your doctor prescribes rest, there's no reason to stop being so active! Contrary to myths, running will not make your baby bounce around inside you, and if your body is already conditioned to handle these levels of exercise, maintaining your workout routine can be the ultimate complement to your pregnancy. That said, this is not the time to pick up any new workouts, and it's definitely not the time to try any contact or potential contact sports like hockey, football, horseback riding, or even skiing.

As your pregnancy progresses, you'll probably notice that you become more fatigued doing your normal workouts. That doesn't mean you should stop by any means, but it does mean you need to dial it back a little. Drop your intensity down to about 60 percent of what you were doing, and then if you still want more of a challenge, increase the duration of your workout. For instance, if you usually hover above the saddle in spin class and go at full speed for 30 seconds at a time, stay put on that saddle (there's no such thing as hovering after a certain point in pregnancy!) and pedal at only 60 percent of your usual speed. If you want to, go for 45 or even 60 seconds to increase the burn. And if you typically love to run outside? That can get a bit dangerous as your pregnancy progresses and your center of gravity drops (as you know from Rosie's story—*oof!*), so instead, try running on a treadmill so you can hold on to the console for a little extra stability.

If you work out a few times a month . . .

Keep up with the workouts your body is used to, but resist the urge to add anything new. If you were a walker, now is not the time to pick up running—but you can pick up the intensity by either extending the duration of your walk by 10 or 15 minutes every few weeks or adding about a 10 percent incline to your walk.

Another great thing you can do is to introduce a bit of weight training to your routine—and since you already have added weight on your body, you don't even have to use extra weights for this! Try sumo squats, rowing exercises for your arms (pretend you're rowing a boat with an imaginary oar, bringing your elbow up to 90 degrees behind you on alternate sides), and modified dead lifts, where you bend your knees slightly and hinge at the hips to lower your torso about 45 degrees before coming back up.

If the last workout you had was in high school gym class . . .

If you weren't working out before your pregnancy, that's no excuse to not be active during your pregnancy—that little baby is counting on you! Start with the basics by just walking for maybe 30 minutes, three times a week. Walking is the template for all other exercises and will definitely get your blood pumping if you haven't been so active in the months leading up to your pregnancy. Don't wipe yourself out with a hyper-fast power walk, but go faster than your grocery-store-browsing stroll. You are trying to break a sweat here!

Other good ideas for beginner workouts are the elliptical machine, swimming and water workouts, and beginner mommy yoga classes. Your hips can feel really stiff during pregnancy, and both the elliptical machine (which simulates walking, but without the impact on your knees), and yoga will help you stretch and extend your hip flexors—and make you feel a whole lot better. And swimming is so easy on your joints, but great for muscle tone and cardio overall!

One-size-fits-all workout wisdom

☑ ABsolutely work those abs!

Not only can you do abdominal exercises during your pregnancy—you *should* do them! Your core muscle group—meaning those in your abdominals and lower back—is what is going to help you most in the delivery room. You want those muscles to be strong. Getting into and holding a modified plank pose, where you get on the floor and hold your torso up with your elbows and knees, is great for this. Remember, this isn't about getting a six-pack, it's about making sure you're strong enough to push that baby out! Just avoid traditional crunches or any other exercises where you're lying on your back. The baby is getting heavier, and his or her weight could actually put pressure on and even damage your vital organs.

☑ Train to lift your baby

It's no secret that babies gain weight as they grow, and you, as a new mommy, are going to be carrying around a (heavy) little bundle of joy very soon. Get ready for that with some simple bicep and tricep curls. Start out with two- or three-pound weights, and go up to five pounds if you need an extra challenge.

☑ Push through your exhaustion to get better rest

So many pregnant women have trouble sleeping at night, and if there's one thing that will help you get a better night's sleep, it's a good work-out. So even if you're tired, do try to get in at least 30 minutes of activity three times a week. You'll feel more rested and maybe even feel your overall energy levels rise a bit over time.

Unless your doctor tells you it's not a good idea to work out, or until you're in the very final weeks before delivery, don't be a quitter. The three pillars of motherhood are strength, endurance, and patience—and it's no coincidence that those same qualities are the three pillars of fitness! As your pregnancy progresses and your center of gravity shifts, it *will* get harder to stick it out, but when that happens, just dial back your routine by 10 minutes rather than throwing in the towel. Your body will tell you how much you can handle, and what's simply too much. Listen to it, but don't give in to laziness. Your body (and your healthy baby!) will thank you.

Prepping your closet to handle some new curves

I have a mantra that I tell all my clients when it comes to choosing maternity fashions: simply put, if you wouldn't wear it before you got pregnant, don't wear it now! Pregnancy is not the time to throw your sense of self and fashion to the wind just because you are bewildered by the growing bump that is wreaking havoc on the wardrobe you've always relied upon. It is just as important now, perhaps *more* so, to feel good. Let's face it, ladies—when we look good, we always *feel* a whole bunch better, too.

I am a huge believer in feeling as good as you possibly can about yourself in pregnancy and in motherhood. When you're happier, it means you'll be better at parenting because you won't be distracted by your own feelings of woe. And I think it goes without saying that a better parent means a happier child, and who doesn't want that? So yes, I am going to link fashion to the well-being of your child and your ability as a parent—a little bold perhaps, but hopefully you can follow my logic!

By the fourth month, if it is your first pregnancy, you might just be starting to show (don't worry if you aren't—everybody shows at a different time). If it is your second or third pregnancy, you probably felt like you were showing from the moment you peed on the stick! Either way, at this point you probably have to put those skinny jeans in the bottom drawer, if you haven't already, and invest in some maternity clothes (no rubber bands around your flies, ladies!).

SMART BITS

Something else that can do wonders for your fitness is a mommy workout buddy. If you've got a good friend or coworker who is pregnant or who already has kids, she knows what it's like to keep moving while the baby's moving around inside you. She'll be an invaluable motivator in the months to come. Add her to your tribe, pronto! Just be careful to pick the right kind of person—you don't want anyone who typically works out way more than you, like Gisele, the crazy workout fiend that she is. A supermodel workout buddy will *not* make you feel good about yourself—but you don't want someone lazy, either. You need a motivator!

The main fashion decision you'll need to make at this point is whether you want to accentuate the bump and announce your pregnancy to the world or hide it, perhaps if you are still deciding when to tell your boss and coworkers. This decision will dictate the types of cuts you go for—tight, ruching details and stretch fabrics or more flowing and loose-fitting empire-waist silhouettes. Whatever you decide, keep my maternity fashion mantra on repeat when you walk into a shop or go online: if you wouldn't wear it before you got pregnant, don't wear it now! And of course, I encourage you to check out my boutiques or online store at rosiepopematernity.com—I designed it *all* for you!

As you head out on your first
maternity shopping trip,
keep these pieces in mind—you'll almost
certainly need them in the months to come:

Pants: Maternity pants of some sort are a must—let your baby and your belly breathe! There are many different types of waistbands, so be sure to try on both under-the-belly and over-the-belly bands to figure out which is the most comfortable for you. Keep in mind that if you want these pants to last for most of your pregnancy, there should be ample stretch in the waistband to accommodate your growing belly. Also, make sure to sit down and see how they feel and be certain they are not digging into you anywhere—especially at the seams. You don't need anything *else* making you uncomfortable right now!

Denim: Once you've established the type of waistline your prefer (and there may be more than one, depending on whether you are going for a more dressed-up versus a casual look), invest in a great pair of jeans. You'll probably spend most of your casual time in these. Most jeans are sized with your "pre-maternity" size, but don't get your knickers in a twist if this doesn't hold true for you. I personally find that my legs, butt, hips, pretty much *everything* gets bigger—certainly not just the belly! When I'm pregnant the "pre-pregnancy sizing," especially in pants, doesn't always hold true. If you find yourself in the same spot, just go up a size and let it go. Buy what fits, and don't get caught up with the letter or number on the label.

Tank tops: Ruched or extra-long tanks are a staple during pregnancy. They are great to layer at the office or at home, and I find them to be one of the most versatile pieces of a maternity wardrobe.

Leggings:

Even if you've never been a leggings girl, they can really come in handy while you're waiting for the wee one to arrive. Do make sure they are thick enough—they should be opaque and have enough elastic that you feel comfortable wearing them as pants without feeling like everyone can see your lady bits!

Dresses:

Dresses can be *über*-comfy while you are pregnant and are often easier to fit into than shirts and pants. They are also extremely versatile, as they are very easy to dress up and down with the addition of an over-the-belly belt, cardigan, blazer, scarf, or some good old accessories. Pick your greatest pregnancy asset—whether that's your legs, your jubblies, or your arms—then choose a dress that showcases just that.

Sweaters (with a little extra something):

Considering a maternity wardrobe is often more limited than your usual wardrobe, look for tops and sweaters that have a little extra detail on them that allows you to wear them both during the day and at night. This versatility will come in handy. I love to look for the addition of stripes, color, embellishment, interesting necklines, or knitting patterns. A special detail takes a basic and makes it shine.

Shoes to lift your spirits:

When all else fails, throw on some wedges (in a bigger size if your feet have grown!) and give yourself a little boost. Heels (even I will admit) can be uncomfortable, especially while pregnant. So to give yourself a little glamorous pick-me-up, *and* a little more stability, stick to wedges. You'll find they propel any outfit, even leggings, into a whole new category of chic.

And now for a few mommy-to-be fashion Dos and Don'ts:

DON'T be afraid of color, bold prints, nautical stripes, and belts that can be worn over the bump.

DO be afraid of too many polka dots, bows in funny places, and tiny florals. You *will* look like you're wearing an apron.

DO try and have fun with your maternity wardrobe. Good maternity lines keep up with the trends, and there's no reason why you shouldn't follow suit. (Unless, of course, the trend is assless chaps. That specific trend just might be a Don't right now!)

DON'T get bogged down in the whole "it's only nine months" mentality! It's *not* just nine months unless you are planning on squeezing back into all of your old clothes the moment you take off that hospital gown. Plus, if you are planning on having more than one child, those months certainly add up!

I do understand the budgetary concerns of having to buy a new wardrobe, which is why I really encourage you to buy a few pieces you love instead of loads you don't. You'll be able to wear these staples over and over and don't have to think of them as maternity clothes, but as clothes you can wear both pregnant and not pregnant. Cut the maternity label out if you have to! You'll be surprised at how many maternity outfits will still work without the bump.

The bottom line is to wear what you like and what makes you comfortable, but don't think that you've suddenly got to "dress the part" of being a mom. Mom jeans aren't a good look on anyone! The only part you should be dressing for is the one you've been dressing for your *entire life*. Yes, as your family grows, you'll grow and change, too— but your sense of style? Unshakable. Now head to the mall, pop online, or check out what I've got in my shops. I guarantee you, you'll find something gorgeous.

The great childcare search begins

As you know, I wasn't the smartest about hopping on the childcare train when I was expecting my first child—and I will *not* let you make the same crazy mistake I did! It might not seem like much of a priority to you now, but finding a private or group caregiver you like and trust can take more time than you'd think—and the last thing you want is to be stuck in a situation where you have to leave your new babe with someone you're not so sure about. And childcare is even important for moms who plan to stay at home. There will be times when you'll need someone to watch your angel, and it's good to have a plan in place before the situation arises.

First, think about what kind of childcare you ideally want and what you can afford. You have three basic options:

- A nanny in your home

- Group childcare at the provider's home

- Day care center

Private care in your home is almost always the most expensive option, with day care centers being a bit cheaper and group childcare at the provider's home being the most affordable. I'm the first to tell you how much I adore a bargain—my sale shopping addiction drives my husband nutso!—but in my opinion, this is the one area where you shouldn't cut corners. You want to think about what it is that will be best for you and your child (Do you want your little one to be in day care with other children so they can learn to play together? Is it important to you to have a caregiver come to your home?), and then budget for that. Not everyone has to have a private nanny, but everyone does need to feel secure and happy knowing that their little one is receiving all the attention he or she needs to be safe, have fun, develop socially, and grow into a bright, curious child.

Once you've figured out which type of care you'll be looking for, ask your friends for recommendations—"word of mom" is often the best way to find someone good—look online for reviews, and then make a list of about 10 to 15 options to call. I know that sounds like a lot, but you may find that some of the day care centers (especially the more popular ones in big cities) have a waiting list months or even years long (insanity, right?!), and finding a good fit can take time, period.

When you find providers with availability, go check them out in person, and if at all possible plan a surprise visit so you can see what things are like when they *aren't* anticipating company. It can be overwhelming to think of leaving your child with someone you're just meeting, so here is a handy checklist of things to look for during your search:

- [x] Is the location easy for you to get to from home or your job?
- [x] Is the caregiver certified in CPR and pediatric first aid?
- [x] What is the ratio between adults and children? Do things seem under control?
- [x] Do the babies and children seem happy?
- [x] Is television kept to a minimum, or at least only watched for an amount of time you feel is acceptable?
- [x] How much outdoor playtime will your child have, and where will this take place?
- [x] Are toys age-appropriate, in working condition, and clean?
- [x] What is their daily curriculum of learning themes for the week, etc?
- [x] What are their procedures in case of emergency?

- [x] How long have most of the staff been working there? Is there a lot of turnover?

- [x] Do the hours match your normal schedule? Will you always be late to pick up your child because you have to stay late at work?

- [x] What is their breastfeeding policy? Is there a comfortable place for you to breastfeed on the premises, and can you bring in and store breast milk there?

- [x] If it is a group day care, what are their sick-child policies?

- [x] Do they encourage parents to get involved in the community and drop in any time, or are they more closed off?

- [x] What kinds of meals and snacks are provided? Are they healthy yet kid-friendly?

- [x] What are their philosophies on discipline, and do you agree with them?

- [x] If you've scheduled an appointment, was the caregiver on time? This could indicate promptness overall or a tendency to run late, which can be a huge problem for busy moms!

- [x] Is the day care or home you're visiting clean? Check the kitchen and bathrooms, and look at the state of the carpet or rugs.

- [x] Do they accept credit cards, or only cash and checks?

Keep the answers to all of these questions, plus general notes on the places you visit, in a little notebook so you don't forget which places were good and which reminded you of something out of a Stephen King novel. Trust me, you may be visiting a lot of these places, and it can get confusing if you don't write it all down! Mainly, though, go with your gut. If a person or place doesn't feel right to you—even if it seems irrational—then it's not the right choice for you, period! Finding childcare is one of the most difficult things to get through and one of the most emotional. You're going to be handing your child over to this person for huge chunks of time! Take your time and do it right. You'll be so glad you did.

It's not ebola, you're just pregnant

Constipation. Dizziness. Nosebleeds. Varicose veins. Headaches. Heartburn. Hemorrhoids. No, it's not penguin flu, or whatever health-scare hysteria is going on right now, you're just pregnant, sweetcheeks. Definitely tell your doctor what you're experiencing in the day-to-day, because some seemingly small things can be warning signs of something bigger, but generally, these are nothing to worry about. The sucky symptoms—and there are a billion of them—are a drag, but it's important to remember that they're just side effects of something wonderful: that little baby growing inside you! Plus, besides the baby you're getting another two Bs that other women have gone to huge lengths to achieve: bigger boobs and a butt!

Still, if you can get relief, you should take it, and I've learned a few tricks along the way. Here's hoping they'll help you, too.

Anemia

WHAT IT IS: A deficiency of red blood cells in your bloodstream, which can leave you feeling woozy or even dizzy.

WHY IT HAPPENS: When you're pregnant, your body produces a lot more blood to satisfy the needs of your organs and those of your little one. Iron helps your body produce red blood cells, and if you're not getting enough through your food or supplements, you can become anemic.

WHAT TO DO: If you feel a bit off, definitely consult your doctor. Anemia (and anything else that makes you feel weird right now) should not be taken lightly. Your doctor will likely give you an iron supplement to take in addition to your prenatal vitamins—but you should make sure to incorporate more iron-rich foods in your diet, too. I love kale chips, burgers, eggs, spinach, and even avocado for this. But it's not enough to simply eat foods high in iron, as it's hard for your body to benefit from it without a boost from a bit of vitamin C. So to make sure your body absorbs all this healthy iron, include something rich in vitamin C in the same meal—bell peppers, oranges, broccoli, and papaya are just a few great options. Even talking about this is causing some tummy rumbles. Time for a snack!

Leg cramps

WHAT IT IS: Seemingly random, shooting pain and muscle contractions in your legs.

WHY IT HAPPENS: This one, so far, is a mystery even to doctors! Some people think it's just all the extra weight you carry around as you get through your day, but nobody is really sure.

WHAT TO DO: If you've got a cramp, stretch out your calf muscle by straightening your leg, flexing your heel, and pointing your toes up to the sky. It'll probably hurt, but it will help the cramp go away. To prevent leg cramps in the first place, avoid crossing your legs, keep drinking all that water, get some exercise, and unwind with a warm soak in the tub before bed—it won't just relax your mind, it will relax those pesky leg muscles, too. Two birds, one bath!

Bleeding gums

WHAT IT IS: A drip or steady trickle of blood coming from sensitive gums. In the right setting, this could make you look like a vampire. Halloween fright fest, anyone?

WHY IT HAPPENS: The increased progesterone levels in your body during pregnancy make your gums more sensitive to plaque and other bacteria in your mouth. That sensitivity can lead to inflammation and bleeding at times.

WHAT TO DO: Brush at least twice a day with a soft-bristled brush, floss daily, and make sure you're keeping up with your regular dental appointments. They're not fun, but they *are* important!

Increased vaginal discharge

WHAT IT IS: A noticeable increase in clearish or milky-white vaginal discharge.

WHY IT HAPPENS: When your body produces more estrogen, as it does when you're pregnant—and when there's more blood flow happening in ladytown, as there is about now—your Queen Victoria produces more discharge, which you might notice in your undies.

WHAT TO DO: Pretty much nothing unless the quality of the discharge changes. If it becomes runny, has blood in it, or is yellow, green, or grayish, call your doc right away. You could have an infection or even be showing signs of preterm labor.

SMART BITS

I know I'm always telling you to drink more water—and that all that H_2O can get pretty monotonous after a while. To keep yourself from feeling too waterlogged, go with sparkling water or grab some flavored waters (just make sure they don't have artificial sweeteners). You can flavor your own water with cucumbers, a spritz of lime, or even by sticking some berries in your ice cube tray and then using those frozen berries in your next glass of water. Just make sure you're getting at least eight glasses a day. You'll feel (and look!) a lot better for it.

Stretch marks

WHAT IT IS: Lines or streaks on your skin (they usually show up on your belly, butt, or jubblies during pregnancy) that can be darker or lighter than your skin tone and are usually a bit of a different texture. Roughly half of expectant moms get them.

WHY IT HAPPENS: When your body grows rapidly, and your skin has to stretch, the layer of elastic tissue under your skin can be affected. When that happens, you might see a stretch mark.

WHAT TO DO: Medical experts say there isn't much you can do to prevent stretch marks, but I've always used stretch mark prevention cream, and I like to think it's made a huge difference because I've never had a stretch mark! That said, it could just be my genetics, which are what usually determine whether or not you'll get these pesky marks. Still, I think the cream is worth it if for no other reason than it will soothe your itching (anybody else out there with dry skin?) and make you feel a little bit pampered. Slather that stuff on your front, your back, and your sides!

Constipation

WHAT IT IS: A horrible, crampy feeling caused by your sluggish digestive tract.

WHY IT HAPPENS: When you're pregnant, your progesterone hormone levels skyrocket, relaxing a lot of muscles in your body—which is good for giving birth, but not so good for, um, dealing with that big meal you ate last night.

WHAT TO DO: To get everything flowing a little more regularly, drink a ton of water—I usually aim for more than the recommended eight glasses a day—and try adding more foods high in fiber like whole-wheat toast, fresh fruits, and brown rice to your diet. Also, if you're not anemic (which I happen to be, and it's lousy!), ask your doctor if it's okay to go on a prenatal vitamin with a lower dose of iron. Iron can make constipation worse.

Dizziness

WHAT IT IS: A feeling like you're off-balance and the room is spinning a bit.

WHY IT HAPPENS: If you've got the spins, it's probably because your growing belly has put more and more pressure on your blood vessels, making it harder for them to pump oxygen to your brain. Less oxygen up in there = one dizzy mommy. Low glucose levels can also lead to this.

WHAT TO DO: If you practice standing up and sitting slowly, avoid super-hot baths and showers (that includes the sauna and steam room, lady!), and have healthy snacks throughout the day, you can avoid this awful feeling more than you'd think. If this doesn't work, and dizziness is still a major issue for you, you could be anemic and need more iron in your diet. Make sure to get that checked out. Eating healthfully can also boost your glucose levels and help you stay a bit more balanced.

Nosebleeds

WHAT IT IS: A drip or gush of blood from your nostril that never fails to happen at the most inopportune time—like when you're giving a big presentation at work or are out with the girls.

WHY IT HAPPENS: The fragile blood vessels in your nose expand while you're pregnant (who'd have thought, right?), but not always enough to handle your much-increased blood supply. Dry air or any kind of minor trauma can make those pressured blood vessels burst.

WHAT TO DO: To avoid nosebleeds, drink lots of water to stay hydrated—I know, I tell you to drink water every two seconds, but I swear it works miracles—use a humidifier at home, and try not to blow your nose too hard. Nobody wants to hear you honk-honking away anyway!

Varicose veins

WHAT IT IS: Alarming purplish squiggles that might start showing up on your legs or in your ladytown.

WHY IT HAPPENS: As your uterus grows, it puts your inferior vena cava—a major blood vessel that runs on the right side of your body—under insane amounts of pressure. That backup can put other blood vessels under pressure (including those in your legs and around your Queen Victoria!), leaving them more pigmented and noticeable.

WHAT TO DO: For a lot of women, varicose veins essentially disappear after delivery, but rather than playing the wait-and-hope game, I'd rather avoid them in the first place. Make sure to get some exercise (check out Andrea Orbeck's amazing mommy-to-be workouts on pages 60–64), try not to cross your legs when you're sitting (I know, I know, I'm uncrossing my legs right now!), sleep on your left side, and put your feet up as much as possible (don't you love having an excuse to do that?).

Headaches

WHAT IT IS: Throbbing, distracting, annoying head pain.

WHY IT HAPPENS: Headaches can be caused by a lack of sleep, dehydration, and even poor posture—which many pregnant women have at least until they learn how to carry their new curves!

WHAT TO DO: Make sure you're getting your zzz's, gulp down some more water, and try to remember to stand up straight. If none of those are working and you've still got a splitting headache, call your doc. In most pregnancies taking a normal dose of Tylenol is just fine, but definitely make sure it's cleared by your doc before downing even those pills. If the headaches don't go away, tell your doctor. This could be a signal of something more serious.

Heartburn

WHAT IS IT? An uncomfortable burning sensation in your chest that can happen after eating, often when going to bed shortly after a big meal.

WHY IT HAPPENS: Acid reflux, heartburn, whatever you want to call it, is caused by the fact that the little valve separating your stomach from your esophagus is relaxed during pregnancy, allowing troublesome acid to seep upward instead of continuing on down.

WHAT TO DO: It's difficult to avoid heartburn entirely, but figure out which foods give you the worst burning, and eat them as little as possible. For me, the culprits included tomatoes, grapefruit, and super-spicy foods—but you'll know what's bad for you to eat in your pregnancy because it'll make you feel just awful. Another helpful trick is to graze on small snacky meals throughout the day instead of eating any big feasts. Your body won't have as much trouble digesting little bits and there will be less acid in your system at one time to bounce back. Finally, it's time to skip those midnight snacks. A few cookies or a sandwich before bed might sound ah-may-zing, but eating too close to snooze-time can cause insta-burn. Make the two hours before you go to sleep a food-free zone, and you'll sleep much better. I promise.

Hemorrhoids

WHAT IT IS: Hemorrhoids are ruptured blood vessels around your back door that can range in size from a pearl to a small cherry tomato. They're painful, and not exactly something sexy to talk about with your partner.

WHY THEY HAPPEN: Straining to go "le deux"* is a major cause of hemorrhoids.

WHAT TO DO: First off, avoid a trip to constipation-land if at all possible. Now, if you're already a walking advert for hemorrhoid relief creams, you'll want to soak your bum in a warm tub at least a couple of times a day; use plain white, unscented toilet paper; and try using extra-gentle moisturizing wipes in the bathroom.

* Rosie, Decoded

Le deux (*noun, singular*): There's tons of bathroom talk in pregnancy, but I've never been one to have a potty mouth—and "poo" is such an ugly word. It even *sounds* brown, right? I just think *le deux*, French for "the two," sounds a wee bit more ladylike.

SMART BITS

You may be that lucky lady who never experiences a single one of these symptoms, or maybe they'll only happen after you have the baby, but most of us go through a bunch of these. Keep in mind, though, these are things that you really don't have to share with everybody. That's right, you can go through all of these sometimes totally icky or uncomfortable things while completely retaining your dignity. The girl you sit next to at the office does not want to hear about your sensitive gums, let alone your constipation issues! In fact, you don't even need to tell your partner every little detail if it's not a medical concern. Some things really are better kept between you, your doc, and *maybe* one other super-close tribe member—like your mom.

Who's in your tribe?

You've already got:

- ○ Your partner and/or your best friend
- ○ Your doctor or midwife
- ○ Your parents and in-laws

And you're adding:

- ○ A mommy workout buddy

Murmurs from the Man Cave

This month, my guy panel has opened up about one of the most dangerous subjects that can be discussed during pregnancy—crazy cravings, mood swings, and other admittedly strange behaviors we tend to have when we're expecting. These guys know us pretty well, and they honestly opened my eyes about what it's like living with a pregnant lady!

Pregnancy can do a number on a woman's appetite, her moods, and just about everything else. Did that freak you out?

"Oh, the mood swings! They were really tough. I tried to go with the flow, but some nights I just had to have a few more beers or an occasional shot to get through it. I knew it would only be a few more months, but still."

"My wife became straight-up weird. I mean, she ate frozen peas straight from the bag! She thought she was handling her hormones just fine. Not so much. There was more stability in a pinball game."

"I was once yelled at because I suggested fruit for breakfast. I'll never forget her screaming 'I DON'T WANT ANY FRUIT!' Mind you, we were on vacation in California—where, um, that's what people eat."

"One night I had to run to the store and try to find her some pineapple at 2 a.m. Not fun, let me tell you. But it was worth it."

The takeaway

I know firsthand how impossible it can be to control your moods and cravings (it's those pesky hormones!), but you *can* control how you deal with your partner. Let him know how much you appreciate him helping you out and being understanding when you get a little testy. Maybe buy him a six-pack of a special beer he really loves and have it waiting in the fridge for him, or treat him to a surprise date night with you and his friends just to say thank you. Whether or not we recognize it, our partners do a lot to indulge us when we're carrying their little ones. Indulge him right back. A little effort goes a long, long way.

Month Five

in it to win it

Mommy IQ:

What you'll be figuring out this month

- ○ Baby's achievements

- ○ Upcoming tests: what your doc is measuring this month

- ○ Mini-me or mini-him?

- ○ What's going on with your body?

- ○ Baby shower!

- ○ Crazy sexy (and totally wacko) thoughts

- ○ Who's in your tribe?

- ○ Murmurs from the Man Cave

{ My **Mommy IQ** is ___ out of 8 }

Regardless of whether it's winter, spring, summer, or fall, one thing's for sure: you, pretty lady, are about to be entering *baby shower* season. We'll get to all the do's and don'ts later on in this chapter, but first I have to tell you about the first shower I ever had, because it—like so many things during this stage of pregnancy—taught me so much.

Of course, since I'm English, the obvious theme was an English tea party. Not that I don't love being British, but I come from a world where a good party is fueled by cocktails and saucy conversation—not a toasty cuppa Earl Grey! I went along with the theme, but insisted on having champagne on hand for my friends—and my amazing mother-in-law who was throwing the party happily agreed. Even with that concession, at the point in the party where everybody would normally be dancing, making out, or getting into naughty mischief, there were my friends, politely sitting in a circle, all "pip-pip-cheerio!" and full of baby talk.

It was one of the most eye-opening and reaffirming moments of my life—and one that made me realize just how much my friends really *were* in my tribe. Here they were, at a party a bit more low-key than they were used to, smiling, laughing, and seeming to have a *fantastic* time because they were excited for me and the baby (and maybe because they were grateful for the bit of bubbly I managed to smuggle in!). I still look back on my first shower and remember how absolutely loved I felt—and will always be thankful to my husband's mom for giving me that moment. It was the first time my motherhood was celebrated in such a public way, and it remains my inspiration for wanting to make every day feel like Mother's Day for mommies everywhere. So put on a cute dress, get ready to open some presents, and . . . let's party!

Rosie's maternity mantras

Hey, sweetcheeks, you've made it halfway through—can you believe it? Take a minute to think about the deeper things this month. Whether you're in the mood for some soul-strengthening wisdom or . . . something totally ridiculous, you *know* I've got you covered. Here's a bit of wisdom I learned from a woman so many of us admire, followed by a good, old-fashioned life lesson (if you can call it that!):

> " It's in the reach of my arms, the span of my hips, the stride of my step, the curl of my lips. **I'm a woman.** Phenomenally."
>
> —MAYA ANGELOU, POET

> " I was always told to be **a cook** in the kitchen, **a lady** in the parlor, and **a whore** in the bedroom."
>
> —MELISSA GORGA, *THE REAL HOUSEWIVES OF NEW JERSEY*

Baby's achievements

Okay, so the Ivies aren't courting your tiny one quite yet, but he or she *is* already quite accomplished. Here's what you should be bragging about this month (yes, I said *should*, because everything your baby does is amazing!).

Your sweet baby is about 10 inches long, roughly the size of a Louboutin pump. That's right, sweets—the Holy Grail. Ignore anyone who compares your wee one's growth to a knobbly old potato or summer squash. Just because it's near your stomach *doesn't* mean it's food.

Watch your mouth—the baby can hear you! Although the little one isn't quite to the point of understanding Shakespeare, he or she is starting to recognize your voice, as well as your partner's voice, and is getting used to your favorite music. In fact, the songs you play most during the second half of pregnancy will probably be soothing to your babe after birth. Some moms-to-be start listening to a lot of Mozart and Beethoven around this time, as it's said to boost baby's intelligence, but why not mix in a little hip-hop? I like to think it boosts street smarts.

Your kiddo's grip is crazy strong right now—think *Superman* strong. (Mmmm, that Clark Kent . . . but I digress.) You could have a future gymnast, baseball player, or golfer on your hands, but for now you've got a baby inside you who can grip its umbilical cord and use it to flip around. *Ouch*. Yes, that was a somersault you just felt.

The most magical thing that's happening right now? The baby is developing his or her own unique little fingerprints. You never needed proof that your beautiful child would be one-of-a-kind—but now you've got it.

SMART BITS

If you want Junior to go to Yale . . . I heard about a woman who bought onesies for all the Ivy League schools and took photos of her baby in them when he was just a month old. Why, you may ask? Years down the road when he's applying for colleges, he can attach the photo of himself in the school's onesie to his application and say, "I've wanted to go to Yale (or Harvard or Princeton) since I was born!" Oh, it's definitely crazy, but I know there's a tiny part of you that's contemplating a little copy-cat action!

Upcoming tests: what your doc is measuring this month

Hey sugar, how are your sugar levels?

In the grand scheme of testing, the gestational diabetes test isn't so bad. Your doctor will have you drink some super-sweet syrup, and then an hour later (bring music to listen to!) will take a sample of your blood to check your sugar levels. If your results are elevated, you will likely be diagnosed with gestational diabetes—abnormally high sugar levels—which could result in your baby being abnormally heavy at birth and having a low blood sugar level once the umbilical cord is cut.

Testing positive isn't the end of the world, because if you have developed diabetes, it's totally manageable. If your results are abnormal, the doctor will have you come back at a later date to undergo a more comprehensive three-hour glucose tolerance test, where you have to fast overnight and then drink the same syrupy liquid as in the first test. In this one, instead of just one blood sample, blood tests are taken both before you drink the syrup and then once an hour for the three hours afterward. If your levels are super high, the doctor may prescribe insulin injections, but in milder cases you'd just need to exercise a bit more, cut down on sweets, and monitor your blood sugar more frequently. Yes, I know, parting with cookies for a while (usually gestational diabetes goes away after delivery) will be tough—but are those crumbly treats more important than your baby's health? Mmm-hm. That's what I thought. Bye-bye cookies, hello carrots!

PAGING DR. GRUNEBAUM

What is gestational diabetes, how exactly do they test for it, and why is it something to worry about?

When you are pregnant, your hormones can affect the way your body processes sugar. In some women, a condition called gestational diabetes can develop. Gestational diabetes puts you at higher risk of having an especially large baby, which can lead to difficulties during delivery and sometimes an emergency C-section. Women who have a family history of diabetes, who have had diabetes in prior pregnancies, who previously had big babies, or who are obese are more likely to develop gestational diabetes.

If your doctor recognizes that you have risks for diabetes, you usually get tested early on in pregnancy, but all women will routinely get screened between 24 and 28 weeks into their pregnancy.

If you have results that show elevated blood sugar after the one-hour test, it does not necessarily mean you have diabetes. Final diagnosis is usually made after a three-hour glucose tolerance test, where, after you have fasted, your blood glucose is drawn; then you drink 100 grams of a glucose solution, and your blood is taken again one hour, two hours, and finally three hours after drinking the solution.

If, after this test, you are diagnosed with gestational diabetes, you will likely be given a special diabetic diet and need to monitor your blood sugars with a home testing kit. If your blood sugars are elevated on the special diet, you may need to start taking medication such as insulin.

The second-trimester ultrasound: kind of a big deal

Get ready—you also have one of the most exciting, and possibly one of the most stressful, tests this month: the second-trimester ultrasound, also called the "anatomy scan." It's an amazing moment to see this precious little person you've been carrying, feeding, and getting to know for months. You love your baby from the moment you know he or she is there, but somehow seeing those little toes and the curve of the lip, and finding out if you're having a girl or a boy (if you want to!), makes everything overwhelmingly real. It's a three-hanky moment in the best way possible.

While this is a time to look forward to, it can also be a really worrisome time for some moms-to-be. The procedure is physically fairly simple—you'll be lying on your back with your belly exposed so the doctor or technician can rub jelly on your stomach and pass the wand over it to get images. Some doctors say it will take about 35 to 45 minutes depending on the baby's position and how much he or she is moving around, but in each of my pregnancies, mine took about an hour. Unfortunately (or fortunately, really), your doctor isn't just checking to see how adorable your newborn will be—he or she is also looking at your baby's vital organ development—such as the development of a working heart and healthy lungs—and checking your baby's growth rate and measurements.

As with the nuchal fold and CVS tests you may have had performed earlier on in your pregnancy, what your doctor sees today in terms of structural development could indicate signs of Down syndrome or other complications. Stressful and scary? Without a doubt. And it's extra freaky because the technician can't tell you a single thing about what he or she is seeing health-wise while the test is being done. All the information goes back to your doctor for review, and then your doctor calls if a problem exists.

I can't tell you how many times, throughout both my pregnancies and IVF treatments, the steely-faced technician left the room saying simply that he needed to "show something to the doctor." It's one of the most horrifying phrases you could ever imagine hearing, and what made it worse is that they often left me alone in the cold examination room thinking every horrible thought imaginable about my baby's health and well-being. The truth is, any "strange behavior" on the technician's part doesn't necessarily mean anything's wrong *at all*. Of course you're in there hanging on his or her every word, because this is *your* baby, and one of the most important things to ever happen in your life. Meanwhile, ultrasound technicians are just people at work, doing their jobs, and they're often not qualified or allowed to tell you what they think. I know it sounds hard to sit there in silence, but try to keep that in mind so you don't overanalyze the technician's every eyebrow twitch or sigh. Focus less on asking if everything's okay and more on how *cute* that baby is on the screen—moving around in all of his or her own glory. And if you can, bring your partner or one of your closest tribe members with you. Having someone you trust by your side will help reassure you if things get a bit scary.

It's also helpful to know that if there is a chance of abnormality found in your baby, you may not be told at this point, or even for a few days afterward. Ask before you leave the office whether they will call only if there's a problem or if they will call either way, so you know what to expect. Then try to put it away in your head for now. I know those days of waiting will feel like forever—like your own personal purgatory that the doctor is putting you through before he or she will tell you what he saw in the ultrasound—but you will get through them. In a way, these moments of waiting, of being freaked out, are great teaching moments that prepare you for being a mom. I can say without a minute's hesitation that I would jump out in front of a bus to save any of my children if they were in danger, but as a parent, you're not always in control of your child's health. You *are* in control of how much love and support you can send their way. Just try to breathe and stay positive, or at least very distracted. Again, you will make it through this. Moments like these are just helping to make you a stronger, better, more incredible mom.

If you are eventually told that something doesn't seem right and you need further testing, it's still not time to get too upset. A lot of my friends have had red flags come up in the days following this appointment, and I can tell you anecdotally that not one of them had an actual problem. That said, if your doctor says something is worth looking into more, that maybe the baby's head seems slightly large compared to his hands, you may want to have an amniocentesis performed. In this test, your doctor will use a long, thin needle to draw a sample of amniotic fluid from around your baby in the uterus to get further insight as to the risks of abnormality. Similar to the role of the nuchal fold scan and CVS that you may have opted for earlier in your pregnancy, this test allows your doctor to look at your baby's cellular makeup to gauge his or her risk of having genetic issues including Down syndrome, cystic fibrosis, and spina bifida. If you want to know more about genetic abnormalities, you can read more about them on pages 238–39 in the Tricky Bits section.

SMART BITS

You know those ultra-detailed "3D" ultrasound pics you've seen online? Don't go into this appointment expecting that your doctor will be taking one of those for you unless you've talked about it in advance. Not all doctors and hospitals are equipped to do it, and since these more detailed photos are very rarely needed to explore the risk of abnormalities, most doctors don't recommend them. Still, if you really want to see a clearer image of your wee one, some doctors will perform them upon request, and there are companies that will take these images for a fee. Just know that the process takes even longer than a normal ultrasound—so think about whether or not it's worth it for you to go through all of that!

PAGING DR. GRUNEBAUM

When my doctor tells me my baby's "risk percentage" for having genetic abnormalities, what do the numbers really mean? What's so high I should be alarmed, and what is so low I should try to put the thought out of my head?

I wish I could tell you there was some "magic number" below which your child would be clearly free of genetic abnormalities, but unless the number comes back as "zero risk"—and it never does—there will obviously be some risk. Typically, however, most doctors and specialists think anything below a one-in-350 chance is low enough to not be overly concerned with—but how concerned you are, and what you choose to do with the information you're given, is entirely your decision, one that you should not be talked into or out of. It's incredibly personal and will be different for every woman or couple going through this. If you are flagged with a high or moderate risk, you will almost definitely be referred to a prenatal center where genetic counseling specialists can discuss your options in depth with you.

Weighty decisions

I just wish I could give you an easy answer as to what to do if further testing points to your child having a serious genetic issue or organ development problems. The thing is, there is no magic solution—and anyone who tells you that "of course you should do this" or "of course you should do that" is simply out of his or her mind. This is *your* baby we're talking about, and thinking about your wee one's health being compromised in any way is beyond difficult. You'll come to your own decision only through discussions with your medical team, your partner, and the people in your tribe whom you can trust to be with you every step of the way. These trials and tribulations are rough; think the situation through and follow your heart. The only right choice is *your* choice—and know that whatever you do, you're already being the best mom you can be.

Mini-me or mini-him?

If your experience is anything like mine was, I'm sure people from all parts of your life have been insisting they "could tell" you're carrying a boy or that "it's obvious" you're having a girl just from looking at you. A very pregnant friend of mine had a random woman point at her stomach and shout from half a block away, "If that's not a little girl in there, then I'm crazy!" Somehow I don't think the gender of my friend's child had any bearing on that woman's sanity—she'd clearly bought her tickets to crazy-town already!

But it's likely not just the mentally unstable who are "positive" of your baby's gender. Even my husband, Daron, claims to have an expert "algorithm" for knowing the gender of a yet-to-be-born baby (see page 95)! Tired of all the guessing? I've got great news for you: you're now finally at the point in your pregnancy when your doctor can determine the baby's gender for sure. The question is, do you want him or her to reveal the big news?

Knowing whether you're having a boy or girl clearly makes clothes shopping, decorating the nursery, and choosing a name a ton easier. That said, my decision to find out the gender of my children had nothing to do with convenience—I just really wanted to know more about the little ones I'd been carrying all that time! There's no rule saying you have to find out now, and a lot of soon-to-be mommies choose to be surprised on the big day. As with almost every big decision in your pregnancy, you should do what you want to do—not what your friends or family are saying you should. This is your pregnancy, and you should run the show the way you want.

For all of our kids, my husband and I wanted to know right away whether we'd be having a boy or a girl—but we also wanted that discovery to be special. Each time, we asked the doctor to write the answer on a card and give it to us in a sealed envelope, and then we would go to the place where we first met and open it together. We thought it would be romantic and make the moment something we'd never forget. And, well, with our second boy, it really was something we'll never forget!

Daron and I met at a rooftop bar in the city, so we went up there, envelope in hand, hoping for the same magical experience. But when we arrived, it had become "boom-chicka-chicka-boom-boom-chicka-chicka" club up there! Neither of us could keep a straight face as we tried to shout over the Lady Gaga soundtrack, and I think the waitresses were probably wondering what a pregnant lady was doing up there, on a date, drinking orange juice in the middle of the afternoon. But when we opened the envelope and discovered that we were having a little boy, we were both just so happy to discover more about our baby-to-be. Even though the place we'd met had changed a bit over the years—and perhaps we'd changed, too—being there really helped make that moment even more sentimental and special for us both.

Whether or not you find out now or on the big day, the thing to keep reminding yourself of is that you're on your way to having a real, live baby. A wonderful, snuggly little one who will smell good (except for when he or she smells not so good!) and smile and play and gurgle and adore you to bits. Boy? Girl? It honestly doesn't matter, because you know you're going to love your child no matter what. Do what feels right to you. As for those opinionated know-it-alls? First of all, it's none of their business—this is your pregnancy, your baby, your decision. Secondly, the way I see it, learning the baby's gender is always a special time, whether at the end of your pregnancy journey or halfway through.

Daron's (only somewhat dubious) baby gender algorithm

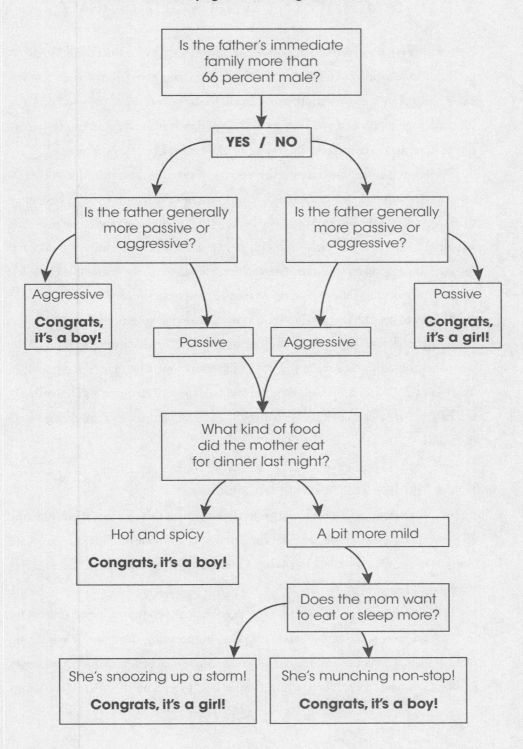

What's going on with your body?

Newsflash: even if you can still sort of squeeze into them, it's time to let the skinny jeans go. Take that elastic band off the button of your jeans, take a deep breath (now that you can!), and go buy some maternity pants. Let the baby belly *breathe*, my sweets! I know it's hard, though. It's as if everything's shifting and growing and spreading even more than before, and . . . the truth? It *is* doing all those things, but for good reason!

The hormones that are coursing through your body, the same ones that are necessary to help your little one grow and develop into a healthy bundle of baby, have more than a couple of side effects. Your belly looks like it's about to explode; you're getting less sleep than a party-all-night club kid; you have Godzilla feet; and weird dots and lines are showing up on your skin. No, you're not turning into the Incredible Hulk, but you *are* transforming into something even more powerful: a mother.

It's easy to get caught up in how you look compared to your pre-pregnant self, but take a step back and realize that this is one of your first big lessons in parenting. If the hormones the baby needs make you puffy or keep you up all night, well then, so be it. You want what's best for your little angel and you know deep down it's all worth it— but let's go over a couple of these changes just to give you peace of mind that you're not alone.

If you feel like you need clown shoes . . .

So, your mom might have forgotten to tell you about this one, but if you're in the 75 percent of women whose feet grow during pregnancy, none of your go-to shoes are going to fit again for a while. Horrifying, I know, but just go with me in believing this is a good thing.

The same hormones that are working to relax your pelvic area in preparation for delivery are also affecting your feet, temporarily spreading them out in length and making them a bit wider. Weird? Yes. A great excuse to get a few extra foot massages and buy hot new shoes? *Totally.* Just do your best to fend off that friend who wants to "borrow" your Jimmy Choos until they fit again. We both know she'll never give them back.

If you're more sleep-deprived than a zombie . . .

The awkwardness of a growing belly, swollen, painful jubblies, increased heartburn, *plus* a suddenly way-more-acrobatic baby inside you can lead to rough nights—but I promise we can find ways to reunite you with your beauty sleep. Since everybody's experience is a little different, here are my top six tricks for getting some shut-eye—try them all until one works for you.

1. Roll onto your side, hug a body pillow, and position the lower half of it between your knees. It's supportive and soft, and will take some pressure off your lower back.

2. Toss out any pajamas or sleep shirts made of synthetics like nylon or polyester blends—since they trap body heat, they'll make you feel too warm and uncomfortable. You'll be much happier in natural fabrics like cotton or silk that let your body breathe.

3. Quit caffeine, or at least don't have any after lunchtime. Some doctors want you to stay away from it altogether, but if you're still sipping lattes here and there, remember that caffeine's stay-awake properties can keep coursing through your system for up to 12 hours, keeping you up when you need rest most.

4. Switch your exercise routine to the morning. The adrenaline rush you get from Pilates class or a jog can function almost like caffeine and keep you awake if you're working out later in the day.

5. Don't go to bed for at least two hours after dinner to avoid heartburn. Lying down after a big meal can make symptoms even worse—ugh!

6. Get to work, girl! If you're up anyway, get back to stenciling that nursery or putting the crib together. You may as well get something done if you can't nod off, and maybe, just maybe, the physical exhaustion will finally get you to sleep.

If you've noticed a crazy line down your middle . . .

This funky little stripe starting at your belly button and going down toward your Queen Victoria is what doctors call a linea negra—in English, that's simply a "dark line."

Some women never develop one, but most of us do. It's caused by the same pregnancy hormones that may have made your nips darker and given you more colorful freckles in the past few months, and it will go away pretty quickly after you've given birth. If you want to keep skin discolorations to a minimum (and have gorgeous skin well into your grandmothering years!), slather on a great sunscreen with a high SPF every day and try to stay out of the sun as much as you can.

Baby shower!

Holy moly, if anybody has earned a party, it's you! With any luck one of your lovely friends or family members will offer to throw you one, because to be plain, it's a bit tacky to throw your own shower. It can't hurt to have someone in your tribe who's fabulous at pulling together events, right? It could be your sister, your coworker, or even your mother-in-law—but whoever offers, be grateful, and remember you're lucky to have people around you who care so much. If your ideal party planner hasn't offered, well, it's fine to tell her all about how totally fun a friend's baby shower was (hint-hint). Some people say flat-out asking her to throw you one is off-limits, but I think if you're close friends, it's completely acceptable. But, if your tribe is worth their salt, they'll be all over this, and so ready to celebrate you and your growing family.

Once you've got that sorted, don't expect to have too much say in what your party is like—it's your host's job to do all the work and your job to sit back, look gorgeous, and enjoy. If she is looking for input, though, here are a few hints that will help make everything wonderful:

- Ask the party planner if instead of a gift to you, she'd be willing to write out two sets of envelopes for attendees—one to send the initial invitations in, and another for you to send your thank-you notes in later. Since she's already going to do up one set, why not two? It'll save you tons of time and ensure you really do get those notes written and sent. If your cousin Gertrude doesn't get a thank-you for that onesie, she *will* be pissed. As the saying goes, don't let perfection get in the way of good intention.

- Have a friend sit next to you as you open gifts so she can jot down who gave you what. Again, this will make thank-you notes so simple you'll have no excuse not to write them.

- Offer guests a choice of bubbly or mocktails to raise a toast to you and the new baby—but you might want to skip the open bar. Nobody wants to scrape a drunky Aunt Myrtle off the floor at the end of the afternoon!

- Urge each guest to bring a book for baby's first library, and to write a note to the baby inside the front cover. Months from now, when you're reading your little one to sleep, you'll be reminded of this super-fun day, and of all the love your peeps have to give.

- Quiz your guests with Mommy IQ questions and award prizes— maybe cute earrings or freshly baked cookies for the winners. Your friends and family will love it, and it will help you figure out whom you can call on when you need a babysitter or a little extra advice.

And here are a few important do's and don'ts for the guest of honor—you!

DO register for baby gear—you need it, and your friends are happy to buy it for you. (See Rosie's No-Frills Gear Guide on page 229 for must-haves to put on your list, and remember to ask friends with kids what they registered for, too!)

DO get something really special to wear to the shower. This party isn't just about celebrating the baby, it's about celebrating *you* for already being such a fantastic mom. Do it up in style—you should feel like a star today!

DO share all the fun and special pregnancy moments you want to talk about. Everyone there is excited about your baby and wants to know how you're doing, what you're loving about being pregnant, and what you're most looking forward to.

DON'T let guests go blindly into the baby superstore without a clue as to what you want and need. They can't read your mind, and they *will* buy you things you don't want (or just 20 of the same thing!).

DON'T let anyone make you wear anything silly, like a paper "hat" covered in gift-wrap ribbons or a larger-than-life baby bib (unless, of course, that's your thing!). First of all, these aren't good looks. Secondly, a lot of photos are being snapped, and you know they'll end up online.

DON'T take anyone's harrowing delivery story to heart. Everyone is thinking about babies, so some people will naturally want to share their own experience—but this is your day and you're creating your *own* unique, unforgettable story.

Crazy sexy
(and totally wacko) thoughts

As you know, I get a little squeamish talking about s-e-x, but there's something we've simply got to talk about: surreal sex dreams. If you're not having them already, chances are these creepy night visions are on their way. Not to give TMI, but the first time I got pregnant, I was told my libido would skyrocket around the middle of my pregnancy—something I'm pretty sure my husband was looking forward to—but nobody warned me I'd be having bizarre, not exactly appetizing fantasies about people I didn't even *like*. It was so icky, I wanted to take a shower every time I woke up (even in the middle of the night!). A pregnant friend who shall not be named had these insanely gross sex dreams—that she wasn't even *in*, mind you—about her old, saggy coworkers. We're talking jowls flapping, wrinkles getting . . . wrinklier. Creepy stuff. And yet, it's what was sexy to her at the time.

You might think you're a bad person for having these dreams, or that you have some bizarro sexual desires that have been repressed for all these years, but trust me, lovely, *none* of that is true. It turns out strange fantasies are totally normal at this point in pregnancy. When our bodies are essentially overrun with hormones, and our Queen Victorias are a bit engorged with blood, it's hard not to think about a little "baum-chicka-baum-baum" when dozing off. And the fact that strange people are showing up in your dreams doesn't actually mean you want to get intimate with those people, it just means your mind has gone a bit bonkers when it comes to getting turned on.

As for the increase in sex drive—some women want more sex, some women don't want to have sex as much as they did before. Everybody's different. Some couples like to take naked pictures when the woman is pregnant; it turns them on. Some people like to have naked "baby bump" portraits painted of themselves. I'm not into any of that—in fact, I barely have any photos of myself pregnant with clothes *on*—but what's crumbs to me is another woman's cupcake. So I won't judge your strange desires if you don't judge mine, but let's make a deal—let's all not hang naked pictures of ourselves impregnato over the fireplace (maybe keep those "intimate portraits" for the boudoir?). And please, please don't leave them up when company comes over—there are some people who just shouldn't be privy to your sexy mommy-to-be photo shoots, including (but not limited to!) your father-in-law and your elderly next-door neighbor. Yes, I once helped a client commission a nude portrait of her pregnant self on a horse, but do I think she should subject her friends and her child's play-date crew to looking at it in the playroom? No. Keep all that stuff somewhere appropriate! It's for you and you alone, after all!

What I'm trying to say is don't feel hard on yourself if you don't suddenly feel like a larger-than-life sex goddess, but go with it if you do. There's no way to predict how your body is going to react sexually to this sudden influx of hormones.

And as for your partner, don't get too upset if he doesn't want to ravish you every time you walk through the door. Chances are he finds your body absolutely beautiful, and he very well may find it irresistibly sexy, too—some men are turned on by seeing their partner pregnant. But then there are guys who aren't as into the preggo silhouette. You know, just because they think it's lovely doesn't mean they want to lick it! The bottom line is that you shouldn't take it personally if he's not all va-va-voom in your business every minute of the day.

Whether or not you're in the mood for sexy times with your partner—and regardless of how he views your new body—*he* almost definitely wants a little bedroom action now and then, and it's in your best interest to go along for the ride and keep your sex life alive. Not that men aren't emotional or that women don't enjoy a little romp just for the fun of it, but I do mainly agree with the statement that women need an emotional connection to have sex, while men need sex to have an emotional connection. We all know a happy sex life is important in most relationships, and this is not the time to let your relationship go down the tubes! Besides, your guy might be going crazy over your fancy new pregnancy jubblies (even though they might not feel super comfortable to you!) and will feel so grateful to get to play with them. So put in the effort. And if your Queen Victoria is a bit too sore for straight-up intercourse, we both know you have a few other tricks up your sleeve that will get the "job" done.

The bottom line is that communication is key—and I don't mean just "body talk," either! Really discuss where you are both coming from so neither of you feels like you have to be a mind-reader in the bedroom. When you're upfront and honest, it's far less likely that insecurities or resentment will arise—neither of which are very sexy at all!

Who's in your tribe?

You've already got:

- ○ Your partner and/or your best friend
- ○ Your doctor or midwife
- ○ Your parents and in-laws
- ○ A mommy workout buddy

And you're adding:

- ○ An all-star event planner

Murmurs from the Man Cave

Here we are, smack dab in the middle of your pregnancy, and smack dab in the middle of the Man Cave! Pull up a recliner or pop onto that ratty couch your partner refuses to part with and get ready to be enlightened.

....

Did you ever want to feel more involved in the pregnancy? If you weren't invited to the shower, do you wish you had been?

"I did want to be more involved, but she didn't really want me at the appointments unless there was a sonogram, so I didn't push the issue. As for the baby shower, there wasn't going to be any beer or any other guys there, so it didn't sound like it would have been much fun to me."

"I always wanted to do whatever she wanted me to and was honestly happy to not attend the shower. While she was there with her girlfriends, I was at home assembling the crib. It was a lot easier without her there!"

"I was a part of every moment. We had a couples shower, and went to every appointment together from the time we started trying to have a baby. So no, I never felt left out."

"My wife talked to me about pretty much everything along the way, and I went to most appointments, so that was good. But my idea of the perfect baby shower is one where I'm not there. I mean, it's not like your 30th birthday party where you invite everyone. It's a party for the mother and her closest girlfriends. That's great and all, but seriously, don't invite me."

The takeaway

Don't assume that he doesn't want to go to appointments, or that he'll feel pressured into going if he's invited. Tell him what will be happening at each appointment, and discuss together whether you find it important for you to both be there. If he bows out, make sure you are okay with that. This is not the time to build resentment and it doesn't mean he doesn't care. Perhaps settle on a few key appointments he'll come to and then reach a compromise on the others. Agreeing on a plan is key.

As for the baby shower, it seems like most guys really don't want anything to do with it (even though they want you to have an amazing time!). Unless he specifically says he wants to be included, let him spend the day with his buddies—or even better, like that one guy, building the crib!

Month Six

mother knows best (or, she will soon!)

Mommy IQ:

What you'll be figuring out this month

- ○ Baby's achievements

- ○ Meet the crib-building elves

- ○ Picking a name

- ○ Be a MomPrep valedictorian

- ○ Touring your hospital

- ○ Want a vacation? Take it now!

- ○ Planning the grandparent visit

- ○ Who do you want in the room?

- ○ Who's in your tribe?

- ○ Murmurs from the Man Cave

{ My **Mommy IQ** is ___ out of 10 }

Sometimes when you're thinking about your baby-to-be, you just *know* how things will be. With my first child, one of the things I was *so* sure of was the name I'd choose if I was having a girl. My nana was the most phenomenal woman. She was courageous and moral, with a truly childlike joy about her. Who she was really shaped who I am today. I knew in my heart I wanted to name a girl after her, but . . . well . . . let's just say her name was kind of old-fashioned, and not in a cute way—more in the way that you *completely* understand why nobody uses that name anymore!

Anyway, I was determined to honor her memory, but I had to figure out a way of doing it without using her first name. Finally, one day it came to me. I'd just name her "Nana." It was perfect—original even! We could call her Nanabelle, which sounds sort of like Anabelle! In my mind, there would never be a more perfect name. That is, until my husband very cautiously told me that I was insane and that there's no way any human baby should be named Nana. I mean, isn't that the family *dog's* name in *Peter Pan*?

Fortunately, my first-born was a boy, and he escaped my insane name completely. I'm not going to lie, though. Each time we have another baby, I do slip "Nana" onto the baby name list just to see if I get a better reaction!

Rosie's maternity mantras

If you're lucky, your euphoric second trimester, considered by some to be a sort of golden window in your pregnancy, should be in full swing. You're past a lot of the initial big changes, you're done feeling so vomitacious, and you've really started to get the hang of your new routines. But you're also not quite so far along that you feel like you can't get up out of bed (well, most days!).

Don't be hard on yourself if you are not feeling completely euphoric, but do try to enjoy that you almost certainly feel better than you did in the first trimester—small things, my lovely! Take advantage and *do* something—set up the nursery, plan a big girls' night out, take a trip, have lots and lots of super-hot sex (okay, I just threw that one in there in case you actually feel like getting jiggy with it. Chances are, you'd rather pick out crib sets, but who knows?). Whatever you do—make it count. A couple of months from now, when you're half-passed-out with a gorgeous little babe in your arms, you'll be glad you did it while you could. Need a little motivation? You know I've got you covered with two of my favorite quotes:

> " Motherhood has a very **humanizing** effect. Everything gets reduced to **essentials**."
>
> —MERYL STREEP, ACTRESS

> "**Baby?** Thank you for my ginormous temporary ta-tas. I promise to **work 'em in bikini tops** until the *moment* you are born."
>
> —MAYA RUDOLPH, ACTRESS AND COMEDIENNE

Baby's achievements

Whether or not you're bursting with energy, this month your baby probably is. That wee one is so determined to grow into a healthy kiddo that he or she is developing at lightning speed.

Baby is finally getting some huggable, snuggable baby fat on his or her frame and will actually double in weight this month. Ahhh yes, those pounds on the scale aren't all you, after all! Your babe is stretching out lengthwise, too. By the end of this month, your little one will be about the size of your favorite fashion magazine (rolled up, of course!).

Along with all of this weight gain, your baby is developing a taste for different foods. Your little dumpling's taste buds have developed, and he or she can now taste the difference in the amniotic fluid depending on what you've just eaten. You might learn whether baby likes (or doesn't like!) different foods depending on the way he or she reacts with kicks or hiccups.

By the end of the month, your wee one will start opening his or her eyes for the first time—and the first thing he or she sees is you! But are those peepers blue, brown, or hazel? Only time will tell—it can take up to six months after birth for baby's final eye color to show itself.

Meet the crib-building elves

Procrastinating a bit on building that crib? The one still in the massive cardboard box, blocking your way to the kitchen? Stop. Right. Now. Remember how we talked about you having no energy to do much of anything later on in your pregnancy, and how this is the time to take care of business? Right. Well, assembling a crib is business that needs to be done ASAP. I've heard many mommies-to-be justify their waiting to build the crib since their wee one won't sleep in it for the first few weeks anyway. But even if you are going to use a bassinet at your bedside to make night feedings easier, trust me that as a brand-new mommy, you'll have neither the time nor the energy and patience necessary to get the job done when the time comes. I promise you, you'll be glad you already set it up when you felt up to it! Now, by no means am I saying you should have to build it yourself. I mean, go ahead and get all DIY if that's your thing, but sweets, as a pregnant woman, you have far more options than relying on your own sweat.

Your first line of defense: your partner. If you've got someone around who's equally committed to this child, and that person hasn't been pregnant for six months, *that's* the one who should be building this for you and your baby. If that's simply not a possibility, or if your loved one isn't exactly talented in the wrench department, turn to other people in your tribe, such as your best friend. Have her over and offer her a cocktail, but don't let her drink it until that crib is standing tall and sturdy! And if all else fails? Here's my favorite solution and something I do every time: when you have the crib delivered, slip the delivery guy a nice tip and ask if he'll put it together for you. Doing a (paid) favor for a nice pregnant lady? Hard to say no. You might want to try this trick for just about everything you have delivered for the baby. Keep a watchful eye, though, and make sure those nuts and bolts are tightened to your Mama Bear standards!

If there are any other big projects to do for the nursery, take care of them this month. It will be lots of fun to add the final touches in the last months and weeks, but the big things like painting and assembling furniture should be done now. If you're painting now, though, make sure you're using VOC-free paint—anything else contains toxins (also known as volatile organic compounds) that may be bad for you and baby!

Spending time in the nursery thinking about all the memories that will soon be made is one of the best ways to spend an evening as you prepare for D-day. Those quiet moments with you and your baby-to-be are truly amazing, and we so often forget to take a break and really think about the miracle that's been happening inside of us. So do all the big prep work for setting up the nursery now—and think of it as decorating for a party or a big event. I mean, is there any event bigger or happier than your little one's homecoming? I didn't think so.

Picking a name

Every couple has a different way of choosing their baby's name. When my husband and I choose the names of our children, we don't look at books or websites, and we generally don't ask for ideas from others. We just talk about it together, and there has always been a name that just *felt* right. The name you choose should be based on that feeling of "just right," which some call mother's (or father's!) intuition. Is the "right" name sometimes also the most popular name at the time? Of course. Could it even be the same name your best friend named her kid? Sure! Neither of those is a reason to shy away from the name that you know in your heart belongs to your child. So what if the neighbor down the street has a little boy named Milo? *Your* Milo is going to be unique and own that name just as much, and for different reasons.

But not all couples have such an easy time coming up with names. Sometimes you and your partner might be on totally different pages. Let's say you love the name Pearl, and he's thinking Shahtiqua. When you realize you're on opposite ends of the scale, talk about what types of names you each like and don't like—and *why*—and then try to find a middle ground. Working together and seeing eye-to-eye is, after all, going to be an important skill in parenting your little one. There will be a ton of things in parenting where you disagree and have to find a common-ground solution. Why not get a little practice in now? So respect your partner's opinions (even if it means your number-one name gets vetoed—hey, it happened to me!) and you'll eventually find a name that you both love.

A final thought to ponder is that the name you give your child has to last his or her entire life. It sounds obvious, but consider the future—when your bright young thing goes to school, teachers will read it from the roster on the first day of class. When your genius graduates college and is looking for a job, this is the name that will be at the top of his or her résumé, representing your child before the interview happens—or before they've heard from you about why your child is the absolute bee's knees and ultimate smarty of the world! The name you choose should be good not just for you at home, but also out there in the world. I'm not saying you need to hire a roundtable of branding executives to help you with this decision—but you definitely want to put some thought into it. Your baby's future kind of rides on it. Hmm. Rides. Ryder. Now *there's* a name . . . see? You can think of really great names when you least expect it if you give yourself a little time to find the right one.

PAGING DR. GRUNEBAUM

So, Dr. G, do you have any suggestions
for what to name a baby?

Of course. I believe the healthiest of all names is a very simple one, one that I know well. *Amos.* Middle name? *Grunebaum.* Lovely, isn't it?

Be a MomPrep valedictorian

When I advocate that parents-to-be take classes to prepare for childbirth and parenting, people ask me whether I think mothers today have lost their motherly instinct (seriously, you'd be surprised how often people wonder about this!). My answer is a very clear no. The thing is, though, we live in different times than the mothers that have come before us. Families are often spread far and wide, and you don't always have wonderfully nurturing matriarch figures nearby to teach you the tricks of the trade. This is exactly the reason why we all need our own tribes! Your mommy friend down the hall will probably know which pacifier is *the* pacifier to have, while your mom may not even realize that there are now 800 options to choose from!

Even if you are lucky enough to have family nearby, you still have to ask yourself whether you think they have the most up-to-date knowledge about infant and baby care. Learning parenting and baby care skills for yourself, be it from books, classes, or other resources, can give you the confidence needed to take on those first few weeks without relying *solely* on your tribe—who may not know all the ins and outs themselves.

I truly believe that knowledge makes you a better parent. If you go into childbirth and parenting educated on basic things like how to swaddle, how to feed your newborn, what to do when your baby is sick, umbilical cord care, and so on, you'll feel empowered enough to really enjoy those first moments, days, weeks, and months with your new little love without worrying so much about whether you're getting the basics right. To be the best mom you can be, you'll want to get prepared. Give yourself (and your baby!) the gift of education ahead of time and you'll both be happier.

I promise, these classes are easy-peasy compared to everything else you've been dealing with so gracefully. Sometimes they can be a little emotional, since they often remind people how much responsibility they are assuming by becoming a parent—yet

SMART BITS

You, beautiful lady, are doing a terrific job—just take a look in the mirror and recognize that you must be doing something right to have that little one thriving and growing inside you. If I could, I'd take you out to lunch to celebrate the awesomeness that is you, but since I'm not there, do me a favor and go get yourself something nice today. That's right—spend a little time, money, or thought just on yourself. Whether it's a gorgeous new dress that makes you feel like a million bucks or an afternoon walk in your favorite park, you deserve it. Being a good parent doesn't just mean taking care of your baby, it means taking care of (and sometimes pampering!) yourself, too.

that, too, will help prepare you. But most important, take these classes so you don't regret *not* taking them. If you ever found yourself in a situation where your child needed CPR, wouldn't you want to be able to jump to his or her aid right away? Um-hm. That's what I thought. So sign up now!

On that note, the class you absolutely must take, and that you should have everyone who might watch your child take—that means grandparents, close friends, and definitely nannies or babysitters—is baby CPR. In that class, you'll learn how to deal with choking, as well as pulmonary and cardiac arrest, in infants, babies, toddlers, and older children. I sincerely hope that you'll never need to use those techniques, but I know that if an emergency arises involving your baby, you'll be so glad you spent that one Sunday learning how to save your child's life.

Another class I find infinitely helpful is the childbirth education and newborn care class. Of course, childbirth can go any number of ways, and there's no surefire way to know what will happen in your delivery until it's happening, but this class will help you understand all of the common variables that might arise. That way if anything unexpected happens during the birth of your child, you'll feel more in control of the situation and less scared of what might be going on.

I know a lot of people are turned off by childbirth education because those classes are known for showing a live-birth video—and usually it's a video that's completely unrelatable to you and your partner. Plus, do you really want to see another woman's child popping out of her Queen Victoria? The truth is, I don't like to watch those either (and I don't really find them helpful; I mean, without a mirror, no woman sees her own child's birth from that angle anyway!), which is why I don't show them in my classes at MomPrep. And if you take a class that shows one, and you don't like it? Just step out during that part of the class. You're a big girl, and this is *your* pregnancy journey. You're allowed to get up and slink out of the room if you like. Nobody's going to ask for your hall pass or give you detention for skipping out on something you don't want to see. Then again, maybe you're curious and want to watch as many births as possible. Either way, find a class and an instructor that feels right for you.

The final class I'd suggest you take is one on breastfeeding. There can be a lot of anxiety tied up in feeding your wee one, and this class will help you feel a little bit more secure in knowing how much your baby should be drinking, and how frequently. And although there is no real way to learn to breastfeed until you're actually doing it, these classes are wonderful for helping you know the signs of when something *isn't* going right. The teachers will give you plenty of resources, including contact information for lactation specialists in your neighborhood. If you can spot a problem with breastfeeding early on, you'll be able to get the help you need (and food into your baby) much sooner than if you hadn't taken the class. Please trust me when I say that it is so important to have these resources at your fingertips. Asking for help is one of the most important skills a parent can have!

SMART BITS

Breastfeeding goes differently for every mom, and how long you breastfeed your child does not determine whether or not you're a good mom—and it can also vary from one child you have to another, as it did for me. Some women love breastfeeding and will do it for a year or more. Other women physically can't breastfeed or have to return to a workplace where pumping is not an option and have no choice in the matter. Still others find breastfeeding so stressful or exhausting that it makes it too hard to be a good mother in other areas, and so they switch to a formula or feed their child with some breast milk and some formula. My bottom line in breastfeeding classes (and, well, pretty much everything else in life!) is that you're there for the facts, not for others to force their opinions on you. Take the good stuff, and leave any and all judgy opinions behind. Do what's right for you and your baby in your unique situation, and you'll be fine.

I do of course encourage you to do the research and learn about the benefits of breastfeeding, and know that some is always better than none.

The American College of Physicians (ACP) recommends six months of breastfeeding, but at the end of the day it's your job to figure out what's best for your baby, and that isn't always as clear-cut as an expert recommendation. I know that you want to be the best mother to that little one as you can be, and that's why I know that whatever decision you make will be a good one.

Planning the grandparent visit

It might seem early to talk to your parents and your partner's parents about when they should come see the new member of the family, but if they're traveling from far away, plane tickets will need to be bought soon, and you want to have a little input as to when everyone arrives and how long they stay.

I can't tell you exactly what will work best for you, but I know having my parents and in-laws wait just a bit before they come is beyond helpful. Those first two weeks after giving birth are simply exhausting, and although everyone will be so excited to see you and your wee one, you might just want to get into your own mommy groove before the grandparents descend. After two weeks of finding your stride (a little, at least!), you'll probably be more than happy to have your parents on hand to help fix dinner or just give you a few hours of naptime while they watch the baby. That said, some people love having extra support right away, especially if they're first-time mothers and don't have a lot of experience with babies. Think about what's right for you.

Another thing to consider is the length of their stay. Even if you love your parents to bits and just adore spending time with them, we all have our thresholds and can take only so much togetherness at one time. Think about what your current threshold is, and then subtract a day or two. That's probably about as long as you'll want your parents to stay when they come to visit. Also important is figuring out where they'll be staying. If they're going to stay with you, an even shorter trip might be in order so that you don't feel overcrowded in your first weeks of mommyhood, and so that they don't end up feeling unappreciated. After all, their insistence on coming out (and probably on staying much longer than you'd like) only comes from the love and excitement in seeing their baby have a baby of her own.

On the other hand, you may find that there's one parent that you want by your side for weeks on end. The important thing, as always, is knowing what's best for you and communicating that in the most loving (and thankful!) way you know how. It's also helpful to ask the grandparents to stay a bit flexible if they can. You still don't know what it will be like in those first few days and weeks, and plans sometimes need to change. It's better to state that upfront than to have hurt feelings later on!

So, take a deep breath, pick up the phone, and have the big "coming-to-see-the-baby" talk with your parents now. Your partner should do the same with his. There may be some hard feelings if your wishes don't line up with theirs, so just make sure you let them know exactly how relieved you are that they're coming, how much you appreciate their help (they really will be helpful, believe it or not), and that you just want it to be the happiest, best trip for everyone. The bottom line is to set the ground rules now. You don't want to have to deal with the drama of different expectations in your first days with your wee one.

Touring your hospital

I so clearly remember my first hospital tour, a few months before I gave birth to my oldest child. I was sure that when I got to the maternity ward, I'd instantly hear a wall of sound—mainly screams and shrieks from women in the worst pain of their lives. That's *really* what I expected to find. When I got there, though, it was so calm and quiet that I almost asked someone where they'd hidden the women! It wasn't *anything* like I'd imagined. And even though that was the main thing I learned during my hospital tour, I'm still so glad I went, and I'm going to tell you to go, too. Knowledge is power!

First of all, a simple tour can put some of your fears to rest (as it did mine), and it's just comforting to know where you're supposed to go. Removing even one question on the big day will make everything so much easier. It's also kind of amazing to see the gorgeous little babies in the nursery. Seeing the teeny bed where your wee one will spend some time for checkups and sleeping while you're resting in your room just makes it all even more real and wonderful. The tour is also helpful because you get to see the rooms, so you can figure out if it's worth it to pay extra for a private room and ask the hospital staff how that works.

This tour is just the beginning of many, many tours you're going to take on behalf of your sweet new love. It all starts with the hospital tour, and then before you know it, you're touring nursery schools, preschools, elementary schools, high schools, colleges . . . and eventually wedding venues! Knowing where your child is going to be will make you feel just that little bit more secure all the way along the line, from (before) day one, all the way through his or her adulthood.

PAGING DR. GRUNEBAUM

Do you really care if your patients take a tour of the hospital first?

By month six, one thing is clear: you are pregnant! And the baby will eventually be born. For most couples that means the delivery will take place in the hospital, on the labor and delivery unit. That brings with it a lot of potential anxiety: Where will I go? Who will see me? What will happen? When will I have to go? What does labor and delivery look like? Many hospitals offer a labor and delivery tour where a nurse or doctor—I do them myself several times a month!—will meet expecting couples and show them the labor and delivery unit. If your hospital offers this tour, by all means take it! It will appease your mind and make it much easier when the big day comes to have the baby.

SMART BITS

You'll probably be on a tour with other mommies-to-be and feel like you need to put some effort into being nice to them—or that you can't ask potentially personal questions in front of them. Thing is? You probably won't see these women ever again, even if you *are* delivering your babies at the same moment, which is a long shot to say the least. So don't be shy—make sure you get all the information you need out of this visit. Got a question about how many moms actually go "le deux" on the delivery table? Ask! Who cares if these women judge you—and chances are, they want to know, too! Anyway, it's not as if you pop out a baby and then cruise on over to your neighbor's room to have tea and share war stories afterward. So sure, play nice, but don't be afraid to dive in and get the information you need. This is an informational tour for *you*, not a test to see how many new friends you can make in the maternity ward!

Want a vacation? Take it now!

With all this serious talk about education, you might be feeling the need for a little break—which is perfect timing! Once you're in your third trimester, travel isn't recommended, because you could end up having pregnancy complications or go into labor early while in transit and far from your doctor. And traveling once you've got that wee one? Well, then you'll have a baby to think about while on the road, on a plane, and in the hotel room. And while adventuring with your child will be wonderful and magical in its own right, there's nothing quite like a pre-parenthood trip.

Excited? Remember, you do need to take a few precautions to make sure you and your baby will be traveling safely and returning home not just relaxed and rested, but healthy as well.

Travel Tips

○ Pick a trip that will be enjoyable for both you and your partner. Sure, your sweetie might love going bungee jumping in Bora-Bora, but that's not exactly the smartest choice for you at this stage of the game!

○ Don't travel anywhere too exotic—I know a remote island paradise might seem tempting, but think of it this way: you've worked so hard to keep this baby healthy for so long, why would you jeopardize that by traveling to a place that may have unclean water that can make you sick? Or somewhere if you were to have a sudden complication, you might not have the best doctors or most modern medical interventions available to you? Stick to developed countries, or just travel domestically.

○ If you're flying, make sure to get an aisle seat, even if you typically like the window. Chances are you'll need to use the bathroom way more often than normal, and you don't want to be the woman asking everyone else to get up 6,000 times during a two-hour flight! Plus, getting up to walk will help you avoid blood clots and help keep your circulation going. Double benefit!

○ Don't eat the food in airports and on the plane. Not only does it usually taste terrible, but these pre-packed meals are also potential hotbeds for nasty bacteria that could make you and baby sick. Be prepared and bring a sandwich, wrap, or some other tasty bit you've made at home. While everybody else is trying to figure out what "mystery meat" they're eating, you'll be thrilled to have something familiar and comforting to put in your tummy.

○ If you're traveling out of the country, play it safe and drink only bottled water. Even if you've heard the tap water is safe, it's better to be overly cautious and avoid any potentially dangerous bacteria that could be in the local water.

○ Reputable, usually more expensive, restaurants are the only way to go if you're traveling abroad. This is not the time for epicurean adventures—if fruits and vegetables are washed in unclean water, or not washed at all, you and your baby could get very sick.

○ Go ahead and take your normal dosage of Dramamine if you're prone to motion sickness. It's totally safe for your baby when taken as directed on the box.

○ Bring snacks. If you're like me, you'll need the little nibbles throughout the day to keep your energy up. Also, when you're traveling, you might not have access to your old standbys and will be super glad you packed your almonds, granola bars, and whatever else you love to keep on hand. They won't take up a lot of room in your luggage and if you don't eat them, you can just bring 'em on back home (but, uh, we both know you'll eat them!).

○ Don't overdo it. I know you're excited to take some time for yourself, but you'll wipe out fast if you try to pack too much into one day. Make sure you've got plenty of time for real relaxation. Some of my favorite vacation memories are of just me hanging out in a bathrobe in my hotel room. I mean, try and tell me room service isn't indulgent!

SMART BITS

Listeria, the super-powerful bacteria that can be found in cold cuts, pre-made sandwiches, cured meats, hot dogs, salami, ham, and even soft or unpasteurized cheeses, can lead to miscarriage or stillbirth. I'm not trying to terrify you, or make you paranoid about every little thing you eat, but I do want you to be informed so you can keep your little one safe and avoid a terrible loss. Listeria is most often found in undercooked foods that get stored in refrigerators, like those in airports and at local fast-food places—which is why I steer clear of both, especially when I've got special cargo on board. That said, heat kills Listeria, so if you really must eat on the go, opt for something cooked hot. It's a much safer bet. For more on what to eat, what not to eat, and food-borne illnesses, turn to Healthy Eating for Two on page 217.

Who do you want in the room?

Another biggie to think about is who you'd really like to have in the delivery room with you. Some women decide right off the bat that they want only their partner to be there; others want an entire entourage. There's no right decision except the one that's right for you, but there are some things to keep in mind while you're planning your invite list:

How many people are allowed in the room?

- Let's say your partner wants every member of his alma mater's marching band there to welcome your wee one with a rousing song (go, team!)—no need to fight him on this one since the hospital will gladly do the fighting for you! Most hospitals and birthing centers have limits on how many people can be in the room at one time, which is both for your benefit (you can do without a brass band—or all those cousins you've met only once—staring at your Queen Victoria!) and to help the doctors and nurses stay focused. Find out what that number is *before* you start making your list, and then put your VIPs right up at the top.

Just because you want someone to be there doesn't mean he or she can be.

- Especially if you're asking people to come in from out of town—say your sister in Toronto or your best friend in Chicago—they might prefer to come after the baby is born or have other obligations around the time of your delivery date. Don't take it personally and don't freak. Just because they can't be there to watch you push doesn't mean they love you any less.

Know why you want each person there.

- Do you want your sister there because she's a mom herself and will be a great help, or do you just feel like you should invite her? Really think about these things, and know what the benefit will be to you, your baby, and your partner before asking anyone to make the trip.

Do the people I'm asking actually want to be there?

- Some people get super squeamish in hospitals, and the delivery room can be a pretty intense place. If any of your invitees seem hesitant, give them an out and tell them it's fine if they can't be there for whatever reason—you just wanted them to feel included in case they wanted to come. It takes the pressure off them and gives them the option to bow out without admitting that they might pass out when the baby starts to crown. The last thing you need is a non-baby-related emergency in your delivery room!

Every invite can be revoked—except for one.

- Make sure that anyone who's planning on being there for the birth knows that you, as the new mom, reserve the right to change your mind at any moment. You might decide that you actually don't want all these VIPs in the room, and that you'd rather sweat out the pains in ladytown without eight pairs of eyes on you—and that's *absolutely* more than fine. You can even ask the doula or anybody else you've hired to step out of the room. It's entirely up to you at any time. The only person you can't kick out is your partner. He has a right to be there, too, even if you get mad at him in the moment!

Who's in your tribe?

You've already got:

- ○ Your partner and/or your best friend

- ○ Your doctor or midwife

- ○ Your parents and in-laws

- ○ A mommy workout buddy

- ○ An all-star event planner

And you're adding:

- ○ Your birth and parenting teachers

Murmurs from the Man Cave

As much as the dudes in our lives like to retreat to the Man Cave to avoid all the headaches of day-to-day life, there's one thing that's unavoidable anywhere you go: money. I got our guy panel to open up about their wallet worries, and gained a ton of perspective.

Having a baby costs money! Were you ever worried about how you and your partner would provide for your growing family?

"Yes, it was a *lot* of stress. Trying to figure out how we'd pay for childcare and everything else—even though we both work—was a constant struggle. Now we're thinking about saving for college, and it makes it even harder. It's been on my mind since day one and it's on my mind still."

"No, I never really worried about that. We're pretty resourceful, and I knew we'd do whatever was necessary to make sure we were okay."

"We had a plan, but we didn't factor in additional life insurance and a few other things, so it was a bit of a monkey wrench trying to actually plan on what we could do for our baby if something happened to one or both of us. I didn't even think of it until a friend brought it up."

"Of course! I wouldn't be a normal man if I didn't worry about money. I'm the only breadwinner in the house, so I worried a lot at first."

The takeaway

Whether or not it's obvious, your partner is likely feeling a bit unsure about how you'll provide for your new family. The great thing about this is that even if he thinks it's all on his shoulders, it's not. You two are partners and you'll figure this out together. Map out the costs of day care, insurance, and even diapers as a team, and talk about what you can each bring to the table in terms of both ways to save and your own earning power. He may still have worries, but at least he won't feel so alone. There are a lot of important money decisions to be made in parenting, so it's a really good idea to get comfortable talking about these things now.

Month Seven

the third trimester's a charm
(sort of!)

Mommy IQ:

What you'll be figuring out this month

- ○ Baby's achievements

- ○ Your birth strategy

- ○ Knowing your parenting style

- ○ Nearly last-minute shopping

- ○ Dealing with your parents (now that you're a parent, too!)

- ○ Who's in your tribe?

- ○ Murmurs from the Man Cave

{ My **Mommy IQ** is ___ out of 7 }

A lot of women start to get a little more emotional as they get closer to giving birth, and believe me, I'm no exception. My husband and I have this tradition of snapping tons of digital photos all year long, and then once a year, we go through them and order prints of the highlights. Well, the year that I was pregnant with my second son, when I started looking at all the moments we'd captured—my growing belly, my son's excitement about the baby he'd soon meet, my husband touching my stomach lovingly—I was sure every single shot was priceless and absolutely had to be printed out. That was 500 photos!

But my crazy brain wouldn't leave it at that. I started to worry that the online gallery we use might shut down or go out of business, leaving us with only that one set of printed photos to remember this incredible year. And then what if something happened to the *box* the prints were kept in? My mind was reeling, and clearly so were my hormones! Finally, I decided that the only rational thing to do was to order *three sets* of my snapshots—adding up to 1,500 prints in full. You know, just in case. When my husband found out, he wasn't too thrilled about the cost, but mainly he just had to laugh. In my own cuckoo way, I was trying to be the best mom I could—I was already doing *everything* I could to protect our newest little son (even his before-birth photos!).

So if you're feeling a little nutso protective lately, just know it's only natural, and a sign that you're well on your way to being an incredible mother. But do take it from me—nobody needs 1,500 printed photos of her pregnant belly!

Rosie's maternity mantras

You've made it two-thirds of the way through your journey, and every little moment so far—the ups and the not-so-ups—has helped to create that precious new little person inside you. Whether or not you think so, the fact that you're even reading this book points to you already being a fantastic mommy, and that's something you should feel good about. It's a rough transition going from being an independent woman making her way in the world to suddenly being totally responsible for a tiny defenseless baby—but you're doing a beautiful job. This third trimester might bring back some of the aches and fatigue of your first months of pregnancy—along with some new stuff—but remember that none of it's in vain. Your body has reasons for the ways it feels, mainly that you're growing a baby—something quite remarkable and impressive, indeed! As you gear up for the last few months before baby arrives, here are a few thoughts to keep you going:

> " Miracles do happen,
> but one has to work very hard
> for them. "

—CHAIM WEIZMANN, THE FIRST PRESIDENT OF THE STATE OF ISRAEL

> " Life is tough enough without
> having someone **kick you
> from the inside.** "

—RITA RUDNER, COMEDIENNE, WRITER, AND ACTRESS

Baby's achievements

I think you know, just from looking at your now much-bigger bump, that your baby is growing a ton—in fact he or she is almost fully developed, and by the end of this month could likely survive outside the womb if you were to go into early labor.

Your teeny treasure isn't so teeny anymore—he or she will have grown to a whopping 18 inches by the end of this month, roughly the size of a large-ish handbag (you know, the gorgeous kind you can't really bear to lug around with you at this point!).

Because of your baby's size, he or she is far more crowded in the womb, and you'll be less likely to feel full-blown karate kicks if you were feeling them before. Instead, you might feel little shoulder and knee jabs. But remember, if you're not feeling as much movement as other pregnant friends, don't worry too much. As long as you don't feel a sudden drop-off in the level of baby's movement, you're doing just fine.

If your partner accuses you of snoring at night (even when you haven't slept a wink), he might just be hearing your baby dozing away inside you. Of course you can't *really* hear him or her catching z's, but your wee one is getting a ton of shut-eye right now, getting ready for even more development—and the big day!

And finally, baby's lungs are almost fully formed and functional. His or her nostril holes will open up this month, too, allowing for little "practice breaths" inside the amniotic fluid. Knowing that your baby is in training to survive in the real world should help *you* breathe a little easier, too.

PAGING DR. GRUNEBAUM

How much should my baby be moving at this point? Is there a way to keep track of the jabs and kicks so I know what's normal and what's not?

Keeping track of your baby's movements is one of the most proactive things a mother can do in this stage of her pregnancy. If a baby is moving too much or too little, it could indicate a problem, so it's important to be aware of what is going on and to be able to communicate that to your doctor.

By month eight, or by 32 weeks into your pregnancy, your baby should be moving at least 10 times within two hours. Most babies will reach that number within the first 10 minutes, but others will take a bit longer. You can track your baby's movements by setting aside 10 minutes each night, preferably after dinner, and going to a quiet place to lie down. Start a stopwatch and then start counting movements. Once you've counted to 10, stop the clock and then record either in an online form or in a notebook how long it took your baby to move 10 times. The amount should remain fairly equal from day to day, and while it normally takes less than 15 minutes for most babies, it may take longer. If movement decreases over time, and specifically, if the baby hasn't moved 10 times within two hours, you should raise a flag to your doctor, as there could be a problem. Some doctors use different numbers to monitor fetal movements, so check with him or her on that.

Your birth strategy

Back at the beginning of your pregnancy, you and your partner should have decided on the type of birth you want to have—in a hospital, in a birthing center, or at home—but if you haven't figured that out yet or need a refresher, go back to the first chapter (pages 20–21) to read up on all three choices.

Once you have your strategy, the most important thing to remember is that it's exactly that: a *strategy*. Things might not go as planned, and you may not be able to have that home birth you'd wanted. Or perhaps you'll get stuck in traffic on the way to the hospital and have to deliver your little one in the back of a taxi. Maybe you'll be ready for a vaginal birth and then have to have a C-section. The thing is, life is kind of crazy, and things often don't go as planned. Even though I've said it before, I'll say it a thousand times because I care about you and your wee one—all that ultimately matters is that your baby is healthy and so are you. Don't go into motherhood disappointed that your birth didn't go the way you'd dreamed it would. Go into motherhood *rejoicing* about that little bundle in your arms, because *that*, at the end of the day, is what matters most!

As you develop your birth strategy, keep in mind the many variables that you might feel strongly about. Perhaps you want (or don't want) an epidural, and maybe you'd like certain music playing at the birth, or you'd like photos to happen only after you and the baby are cleaned up a bit. Talk all of these issues over with your partner and your doctor to make sure everyone is on the same page. This step is so important—your partner can help advocate for your plan if you're unable to, unless of course circumstances have changed and your plan is no longer practical. Once you're set on your full strategy, go ahead and write it down so nobody forgets in the moment, but remember that no matter what you'd like to happen, the two biggest priorities on that day are your *baby's* health and safety and *your* health and safety. If, in the moment, a nurse forgets to start your music because she was too busy making sure your baby was positioned the right way for a safe delivery, chill and be grateful that the professionals around you know what they're doing. Hearing Taylor Swift during that final push can't safeguard your baby's health, but the expertise of doctors and nurses surely can.

I know it's tough, and you'll want to feel as comfortable as possible going into something so scary, but there is a time to put our own personal preferences aside in favor of making the smartest, safest decisions for our children. You've been doing that all along by giving up some of your vices, eating right, finding the right balance of exercise, and generally taking amazing care of yourself and your precious babe. How you strategize your delivery is just an extension of that. Be smart, think safe—that should be every mommy's motto from *before* day one.

You already know my mantra: do what's best for your baby, because that's what it means to be a good parent.

Know your parenting style

There are as many ways to raise a child as there are ways to wear a little black dress, and now is the time to make sure you and your partner are on the same page when it comes to what kinds of parents you're going to be. Do you want to be strict or more lenient? Do you want to raise your child in a specific religion? If you're a vegetarian, do you expect your child to be one as well? What are the decisions that you'll leave for your child to make for him- or herself later on? Are you co-sleeping? Do you believe in "time out"? I know it seems like I'm getting ahead of myself, but aligning your parenting philosophies now can help you avoid misunderstandings and conflict later on.

Chances are, as your child grows, you will change your minds about more than a couple of things you talk about now in your parenting discussion. As you grow as a parent, you'll learn what works and doesn't work in terms of your unique little one—but having a solid foundation from the start will give you a core set of values to work with, and more stability in general at home.

Some of the most common questions I get are about how pregnancy and raising children affects relationships, whether it's about agreeing on how to save and spend money as parents, parenting philosophies, sex—you name it, I've heard it! My answer is always the same, and it's best to know it and live by it now: communication. No matter how hard it gets, you've got to talk things out respectfully and find a common ground with your partner and your tribe. With some practice (starting now!), you'll make it through this as a great team.

Nearly last-minute shopping

If you're like—oh, let's just say most women I know, right now you're thinking you won't go into labor for a few more months, so you have plenty of time to kick back and leisurely cruise through all the baby stores on Sunday afternoons with your best girlfriends, picking up some tiny socks here, a little pack of diapers there. And while those Sunday Fundays sound simply yummy, they are *not* the way to go, lovely.

The reality is that you could go into labor much sooner than your due date, and the baby could arrive not just days, but weeks or even *months* before he or she was expected. Think about it this way: you probably keep a bottle of wine and at least minimal snacks in the house in case guests drop by unexpectedly, right? Why on earth wouldn't you do the same (with different provisions, of course!) for your child?

You simply don't want to be caught without the essentials. Diapers, diaper cream, receiving blankets, baby wipes, easy-on-and-off outfits for baby, easy-on (and washable!) outfits for you, formula and bottles if you're not breastfeeding, a car seat, and a stroller or baby sling are all things you really must make sure you have on hand, right now. Go to my No-Frills Gear Guide on page 229 for a full list of stuff you'll need before that baby gets here. I can't say this enough—get all of this stuff out of the way so that you can enjoy the big moment without having to freak out over whether or not you have the little things your little one needs.

You can make all of this shopping easier by hopping online and ordering everything with the push of a button. In a few days you'll have everything you need at your fingertips, and you'll feel so much more confident being able to take care of all your wee one's first needs—no matter *when* he or she arrives.

Dealing with your parents (now that you're a parent, too!)

You've done the thinking, you've done the strategizing, you've done the parental philosophizing—and now your parents or his parents are poo-pooing all of your ideas on how you want to raise this baby.

The tricky thing is that they think they know everything because they've done it before—and in a way, that's true; I mean *you* turned out okay, right? But that still doesn't give them the right to tell you what kind of parent to be. Talk to your parents (and have your guy talk to his) and go over what you guys decided on in terms of how you want to parent your little one.

Tell them that you totally appreciate their help and are so grateful that your baby is going to have such amazing grandparents—but also request that they wait to offer advice until you've asked for it. You'll ask for it plenty (you really will, even if you think you won't), but when you're busy diapering a fussy baby or half asleep after a long night, their unprompted two cents will just go in one ear and out the other, no matter how valuable what they have to say really is. (It also will probably make you more than just a little annoyed—but you don't need to tell *them* that.) If they wait to offer solutions until you've asked for help, they'll know you're really listening and ready to get the most from what they've got to offer. See? Everybody wins. But you have to remember to ask for help. This whole thing *only* works if you ask!

Try to remember that your parents may actually be able to help, so try—just try—and ask their opinions once in a while, even if you ultimately *don't* take their advice!

Who's in your tribe?

You've already got:

- ◯ Your partner and/or your best friend
- ◯ Your doctor or midwife
- ◯ Your parents and in-laws
- ◯ A mommy workout buddy
- ◯ An all-star event planner
- ◯ Your birth and parenting teachers

And you're adding:

- ◯ You! Remember, you still exist and *you* need *you* (and so does your baby!).

Murmurs from the Man Cave

When you look in the mirror, chances are, you're blown away by the difference in the way you look and carry yourself now. Don't think your partner hasn't noticed, too! I crept down to the Man Cave to see what they had to say about your new curves and was totally surprised by their comments. Come have a listen.

Pregnancy totally changes a woman's body. What did you really think about the way she looked in her third trimester?

"One of my friends said pregnancy was the only time in a married man's life when he can optically cheat on the lady he married. I mean, I don't feel this way at all, but he says you can turn off the lights when the woman you love is pregnant and pretend she's a totally different lady, because she *feels* different!"

"She was still beautiful. The glow women have during that time is like nothing else."

"Yeah, her boobs do get big and you're like, 'Whoo-hoo, yes!,' but then they also get super sensitive and you're told they're off-limits. So they're fun to look at, but that's pretty much the end of it."

"I'm really conscious about my body. Like, am I gaining weight because I'm eating too much or am I getting skinny and need to eat more steak? That's me. But her? Her body *has* to change so the baby can grow. I have a lot of respect for that—I could never give up that much control."

The takeaway

Men are so often simply in awe of the fact that we can grow babies inside us that even though they notice how our bodies change, they're mainly just focused on the positives—*hello* jubblies! That said, your partner acknowledges that your body is different, and how hard that may be for you. Don't be too hung up on your changing body, and remember he loves you more now than perhaps ever—you are the mother of his child. Plus, chances are he really wants to be intimate with you, so take his lead and remember how beautiful you are.

Month Eight

you're really almost there!

Mommy IQ:

What you'll be figuring out this month

- ○ Baby's achievements

- ○ It's not bubonic plague, you're just still pregnant

- ○ The doc's office as your second home

- ○ Breastfeeding: the ins, the outs, and the leaky bits

- ○ Prep everybody else for the baby

- ○ Finding a pediatrician

- ○ Wrapping up at work

- ○ Early contractions—nothing to sneeze at!

- ○ Birth announcements

- ○ Strategy check-in

- ○ Who's in your tribe?

- ○ Murmurs from the Man Cave

{ My **Mommy IQ** is ___ out of 12 }

Month eight is one of those points in pregnancy that can feel extremely different for different people. Some mommies-to-be cannot fathom how fast the time has gone by and how quickly their baby has grown. If you fall into that camp, I totally understand you wanting to savor every experience and make each moment last. On the flip side, there are women who are just plain old tired (because, um, becoming a mom can be exhausting!) and beyond eager to make this last segment of the pregnancy zip by.

However you're feeling, the truth is you're just weeks away from mailing out baby announcements to all of your loved ones. Surreal, right? If pre-addressing tiny envelopes sounds a bit overwhelming, and you'd rather just let someone else deal with it while you rest—go ahead, but let my experience be a cautionary tale!

Near the end of my first pregnancy my husband sweetly offered to handle all the birth announcements, saying that I already had enough to think about. Exhausted and so grateful, I accepted his offer without hesitation. We had already chosen these precious little cards with a blue elephant on each one, so I figured all that was left was for him to add the baby's name, weight, height, and birth date and pop them in the mail. Nothing could go wrong, right? Wrong!

When I finally saw one of the cards my loving husband had sent out to all our nearest and dearest, I nearly keeled over. I read with horror that it not only stated our son's name, date of birth, weight, and length—but it also said, in huge letters, "I can't wait to pee on you!" Obviously, Daron thought this was hilarious, but I . . . well, let's just say I would have been a bit more *conservative*.

The lesson I learned, and that I hope you take from this, too, is that you absolutely *should* accept help right now. But for the important things, definitely make sure you have final approval!

Rosie's maternity mantras

You're almost, and I mean *really* almost, there—that wonderful day when you can hold your precious babe is just a couple of weeks away. This is a time in pregnancy when (I've found, at least!) a lot of people are trying to tell you how you should feel. "Aren't you so excited?" a nosy coworker will squeal, when really you've been having recurring stress dreams about what the delivery will be like. Or, better yet, a neighbor will offer, "My sister-in-law was in labor for *three days*! What if that happens to you?" on a day when you're finally feeling confident and like everything's under control. If you're a little more on edge than usual and unsure as to what is ahead, or if you can't *wait* for the days and weeks to fly by, trust me, it's all 100 percent normal.

Having a baby—a real-life, breathing, blinking, snuggling, *outside-of-you* baby—is a huge change to go through, and as you get closer and closer, you might find yourself needing a few more distractions to either make the time go by faster or keep your mind off some of the stuff that's outside your control. (And remember, as a parent *so much* of your little one's life will be outside your control—these feelings you're having now are just prepping you to be a good mommy later on!) If you've taken my advice, though, and prepared and educated yourself along the way, try to take some (if not loads of) comfort in the fact that you are absolutely as prepared as you can be. I promise when you hold that wee one in your arms, you'll know just what you need to do—love him (or her)!

For now, try catching up on some movies you didn't feel well enough to see during your first trimester (The good news? You can get them On Demand now!), call a friend you've been meaning to catch up with, or basically, take some time to do anything that doesn't have to do with your upcoming delivery day—but that has everything to do with you. There won't be a lot of you time in the months ahead. Focusing on things other than the birth will make the next few weeks a whole lot easier, I promise. In the meantime, here are a few thoughts you might be able to relate to:

> " Adopt the pace of nature:
> her secret is **patience.**"

—RALPH WALDO EMERSON, WRITER AND POET

> " The **suspense is terrible.**
> I hope it will last."

—OSCAR WILDE, WRITER AND POET

Baby's achievements

I know, it might not seem possible that you could hold anything bigger inside you, but your baby still has a bit of filling out to do. As your wee one starts to feel more crowded in the amniotic sac, it will be harder for him or her to find a comfy position, which can lead to a bit more kicking and stretching.

Just three months ago, your baby was the size of a classic stiletto, but now he or she has stretched out to a whopping 20 inches—roughly the length of your favorite fall boots! This is about as "tall" as baby will get until after birth, but your tiny one will keep packing on the pounds until the day he or she arrives.

Your babe is already building up a defense system against all the icky germs that could get him or her sick outside the womb. By taking antibodies from your system, he or she is developing a strong immune system that will try to keep the sniffles at bay.

That genius brain just keeps on getting bigger and smarter, leading baby to have a head that's a little large in proportion to the rest of his or her body. If you're lucky, that big head will be pointed downward at this point, which will make for an easier vaginal delivery—but if it's pointed upward or to the side, your doc can suggest exercises to urge that head down south. (And so will my doc—see his box on baby positioning below.)

PAGING DR. GRUNEBAUM

What does it mean if my baby's in breech? Can I make my baby move to be in the best position for giving birth?

It's normal for the baby to be in breech until about two months before your due date, and most babies will turn around by that time. However, about one in 30 babies will be positioned with the head in the upper part of the uterus and the butt down, which is called "breech" toward the end of the pregnancy. In the United States, the vast majority of doctors will not recommend vaginal delivery if a baby remains in breech because there are risks to the baby, including physical injuries, that can happen when a breech baby is born vaginally.

If your doc finds out your baby is breech there are two choices. The doctor can recommend a scheduled C-section after 39 weeks or discuss a procedure called "external version" with you. This procedure, which is usually done between 37 and 40 weeks of the pregnancy, is where the baby is physically turned around into a vertex, or head-down, presentation. It can only be done before you are in labor and before your water has broken. For this procedure, you would go into your doctor's office or the hospital and the doctor would physically dig his or her hands into your abdomen to grab the baby's head and butt and rotate its position so it ends up head-down. It's like a very strong massage on the abdomen and can feel uncomfortable, but can drastically reduce the need for C-sections. This does not hurt your baby, but your doctor will continue to monitor the baby's health and position after the fact to make sure the umbilical cord did not get compressed during the procedure.

What if we can't get the baby to move? Will we both be okay?

Yes. If the baby cannot be moved for one reason or another, your doctor will almost definitely indicate a C-section. Although there are more risks involved to the mother with a C-section than with a vaginal birth, this is one of the situations in which a C-section is far safer for your child than a vaginal delivery would be.

It's not bubonic plague, you're just still pregnant

If you're feeling not-so-fabulous lately, but can't figure out what's going on, there's probably no reason to panic. It's pretty common for some or all of the uncomfortable pregnancy symptoms you dealt with in the first trimester (like a champ, I must say!) to pop back up near the end of your pregnancy.

I want you to feel your strongest and most capable right now, so refer back to pages 73–78 for a quick list of what you might be going through and what you can do to start feeling better fast. And remember, your body isn't trying to torture you, it's just doing what's necessary to create your gorgeous little son or daughter. And that, no matter *how* gross you might feel right now, is more than worth it.

Above all else, always tell your doctor what's going on with you. Even if you're pretty sure it's no big, you'll rest better at night (and you need your sleep, sweets!)

after hearing that everything is A-okay from the person who knows best. I find that as women we can often be too stoic. Your doctor is there to help, and I hope that by now you've been to see him or her enough times that you've formed a healthy relationship. So use this support by telling your doctor your concerns and asking all of your questions. Keeping your anxiety to yourself isn't good for you or the baby.

The doc's office as your second home

Near the end of your pregnancy, you may as well have your mail forwarded to your doctor's address. Around the eight-month mark, many doctors will want to start seeing you every two weeks to check your health and the baby's progress. If your pregnancy is high-risk or has already started having complications, you may need to go into the office even more frequently.

All of this back-and-forth can be frustrating (you want me to hop into the car *again?*), extremely comforting (baby's heartbeat's still going strong!), or a combination of both; so I have a couple of tips to help make every trip a little more pleasant:

- **Make friends with the nurses.** Remember their names, and even think about treating them to coffee or pastries one day. They'll remember the gesture and be more likely to give you a little extra-nice treatment when you need it most. Trust me, I've shown up unannounced on more than one occasion at my doctor's office and the nurses were amazing while I waited. It's important to recognize and appreciate your baby's team!

- **Pick something extra juicy to read that will take you a long time to finish**—and save it just for doctor appointments. Or start writing letters to your baby-to-be from the waiting room and then send them all to a dedicated email address that you can show your son or daughter in the years to come. Both will give you something to look forward to and can turn the waiting-room wait from humdrum into actual fun.

- **Bring a snack.** I know you're weary of me drilling it into your head, but unless your doc asks you to fast for a test (which would be rare at this point), you'll want to keep your blood sugar at a good level so you're not tempted by the drive-thru on the way home. Toss some almonds into your bag and you're good to go. Besides, you know as well as I do that the food at the hospital cafeteria doesn't exactly come from yummycakes island!

Breastfeeding: the ins, the outs, and the leaky bits

I hope you've been showing off those lovely jubblies, lady, because they deserve to be celebrated! Not only have they given you a sexy new silhouette, they're also going to be full of super-healthy milk for your baby.

If you know you would like to breastfeed or are starting to think about it, I strongly recommend learning as much about it as possible before the baby comes. For some women, breastfeeding can be an incredibly easy thing, but for many it can be very difficult at first and, in my experience, can be a major cause of emotional stress in the first days after the baby is born. Having said that, if you master breastfeeding it can be one of the most amazing and rewarding experiences for you and your baby.

Breastfeeding is a deeply personal choice, and I ask that you not judge people for making a choice that differs from yours. There are many factors that go into deciding whether breastfeeding or formula feeding is right for you and your baby, and this choice—like everything else in your journey—should be made based on your unique situation. I do encourage everyone, however, to learn about the benefits of breastfeeding and, if possible, to give it a try. As they say, if you can, some is better than none.

It's also important to remember that breastfeeding is a learned skill that can take patience and perseverance, so you should have a support system on hand just in case it's not as easy as you'd hoped it would be. And don't be afraid to use that support system. It's important to ask for help early on, before breastfeeding becomes too painful (it can really hurt if it's not going well) and your baby gets too hungry.

I have put together some tips and tricks for breastfeeding, but they are no substitute for taking a class, locating a lactation consultant in your area to have on speed dial, and finding support groups just in case you need them. But if it turns out that breastfeeding doesn't work for you, or you simply cannot do it for other reasons such as medical, work, or supply situations, then please, *please* remember it does *not* make you a bad mother. The choice to breastfeed is personal for every family and can be different with each child, as it has been for me.

Weighing the pros and cons of breastfeeding will be different for each person, but as long as you have your baby's best interests at heart when you make the decision you *are* making the right choice for you and your child, given the bigger picture.

And now on to the great things you should know about breastfeeding. Some benefits:

- It helps to support the baby's immune and digestive systems.

- It promotes mommy–baby bonding.

- It can help you lose weight faster as it speeds up your metabolism, shrinking your uterus and burning roughly 500 calories a day (the same as a 45-minute spin class!).

- It's definitely cost effective.

Breastfeeding timeline

In the weeks leading up to the birth of your baby, you will probably notice a yellow or goldish sticky substance on the inside of your bra. This is the start of your breasts' colostrum production, which comes before your milk supply is in. Colostrum is incredibly nutrient and antibody rich, low in fat, and high in carbs and protein, which makes it perfect for your baby when he or she is first born.

It takes approximately three to five days for your breast milk to come in, so you will be giving your baby colostrum in those first few days after birth. When the milk finally does come in, your breasts will swell and almost certainly feel engorged—they can each get up to 1½ pounds heavier, so there is really no missing it! Because the milk supply often doesn't come in until after you've left the hospital or birthing center, it's important to have those support numbers on speed dial. The hospital lactation consultants may no longer be at your fingertips at the point when you finally need them.

Here's how it works: when your baby sucks at your breast, signals are sent to your brain, which in turn signals the release of hormones that cause the body to make and release milk. So the more you breastfeed in those first days, the more it will help your milk supply along. The more milk your baby takes out, the more you make. Your breasts work on a supply-and-demand model, so to keep making enough milk it is important to keep up the breastfeeding. Ultimately, this will work in your favor when you want to stop breastfeeding. As you reduce the amount you breastfeed and the amount of milk your baby drinks, the amount you make will gradually diminish, too.

The importance of a deep latch

I can't stress enough how important it is to make sure your baby has a proper latch on your breast. If the latch isn't correct, it can be the source of a lot of pain and discomfort, and ultimately is why many women stop breastfeeding. So be sure to take advantage of the expertise available where you give birth to check that your baby has a good latch. Hospitals often have lactation consultants available, and doulas and midwives can also be incredibly helpful.

When trying to achieve a good latch, remember these things:

- Don't push your baby's head into your breast, but instead support the neck and back of the head and bring the baby close to the nipple, then allow your baby to reach forward and match the latch.

- You can help your baby to open his or her mouth wide by stroking the baby's cheek or circling with your finger around the baby's lips. It can also help if you hold your breast with the nipple pointing forward. However, a newborn baby lying on his or her mother's chest will actually be able to find the nipple independently.

You know you have a good latch when:

- Your baby's mouth is wide open and lips flared out, with his or her chin touching your breast.

- You can see more of your areola above your baby's top lip than below the lower lip, as opposed to your baby having only the nipple or a small amount of breast in his or her mouth.

- You can see his or her jaw move as your baby takes long, drawing sucks.

- You can hear your baby have several periods of active sucking and swallowing during the feeding.

- You can feel a strong tug that is not painful. It may start out with discomfort in the beginning days of breastfeeding, but it is *very* important that this goes away during the feeding and does not get worse. If it gets worse, then there is something wrong with the latch.

Feeding positions

There are many different positions in which you can breastfeed your baby. Finding what's best and most comfortable for both of you might take a few tries, so definitely experiment with a few different holds until you discover what works. Some may work better at different times of the day or be better for different environments and situations. Here are some common holds that mothers and their wee ones often find comfortable:

Cradle

Cross-cradle

Football

Side-laying

How do I know my baby is getting enough milk?

Many women worry that their baby isn't getting enough milk in the first days after giving birth before their milk supply comes in. It is important to remember how small your baby's stomach is when he or she is born—a newborn's stomach can hold only one to two teaspoons of fluid at a time! But it is also important to keep tabs on whether your baby is getting enough milk. Here are some ways to tell that your baby is getting enough food:

- Your baby is having enough wet and dirty diapers.

- Your baby seems calm and full after feedings.

- Your breasts feel softer and lighter after feeding your baby.

Your baby should be gaining weight after the initial expected weight loss immediately after birth. Some mothers like to use a baby scale to know how much milk the baby is getting. You can weigh the baby before and after feeding, and the difference between the two is roughly how much milk he or she is getting.

Your newborn should feed about 8 to 12 times every 24 hours—doing the math, that calculates to once every two to three hours. Don't worry if your baby isn't on a regular schedule to start. You may find at first the baby will feed every hour, take a longer break, then feed again after four hours. The two important things to remember are that you shouldn't go much longer than four hours between feedings with your newborn and that over a 24-hour period, the baby is having those 8 to 12 feeds. Gauge the time between feedings from the beginning of one feeding to the beginning of the next, not from the time you stop feeding.

It's also important to split the feeding between both breasts. Try doing 15 minutes on one and then 15 minutes on the other, and extend the time as the baby needs more. This time can be very variable, and some babies will want to feed for much longer on each breast. Be sure, however, to remember (write it down, or use a bracelet on that arm to remind you) which breast your baby fed on last so that you begin your next feeding on the other breast to try and regulate as close to an even milk supply as possible.

Ideally, you and your baby will get into a rhythm and schedule so your baby is fed before getting so hungry he or she cries. Sometimes this doesn't happen, and crying can be a sign of hunger. Some other signs to look for include smacking or licking lips, opening and closing the mouth, sucking on hands, fingers, toes, or clothing, hitting you on the chest (*ow!*), and fussing or breathing really fast.

If you think your wee one isn't getting enough milk, your latch is too painful, you notice painful engorgement of your breasts, or you have cracked or even bleeding nipples—for goodness' sake, put down this book and call your lactation expert! These experts are there to help you. Let them do their job, and you and your babe will be much happier.

SMART BITS

I find women often think they either breastfeed or they don't—but breastfeeding is absolutely not an all-or-nothing thing. Sometimes breastfeeding and formula feeding can work together brilliantly—for example, if you are working during the day and are not pumping enough to store for the full day. Just because you introduce some formula doesn't mean you have to stop breastfeeding altogether!

Bonding like crazy during bottle feedings

Anyone who says breastfeeding is the only way to bond during feeding is not correct. Yes, breastfeeding can be an amazing experience, but so can bottle-feeding when breastfeeding is not possible! Whether you plan on using bottles for formula or breast milk, you can absolutely get a ton of closeness during feeding times. Here are a few quick tips to help you make every moment with your little one special:

- Find a warm, quiet place to do most of your feeding (sometimes you'll be places that aren't perfect, and that's okay!).

- Find a bottle that works well for your baby. Slow-flow nipples are the most similar to the breast, but it might take some trial and error to discover what works for the two of you.

- Alternate holding your baby in your right arm and left—it will keep your arms from getting too tired, so you can really relax, and will help keep the baby from having a slightly flatter head on one side.

- Establish skin-on-skin contact while bottle-feeding. That's right—take off that hoodie for some intimate cuddles!

- Go ahead and let in-laws and friends lend a hand once in a while (heaven knows a break will be nice now and then!), but don't let them take over completely. How is baby going to bond with you if you're rarely the one with the bottle?

- Just as with breastfeeding, don't talk on the phone, watch TV, or do almost anything else while giving your little one a bottle. Talk to your baby, sing, explain all your hopes and dreams, and—most of all—tell your baby you love him or her. Enjoy the quiet; these moments are precious. Don't waste them!

Prep everybody else for the baby

Breaking news: your babe is not coming into an isolated world where he or she will interact with only you and your partner. In fact, your baby will be meeting a whole host of characters, and the more you prepare all of those people (and pets!) for the arrival of your little one, the smoother everything will go.

The babies you've *already* had

If you already have kids, you've probably fielded plenty of questions about mommy's belly and whether you're giving the family a little brother or a little sister. Even if you've told your children that they're going to have a new sibling to love and care for, it's completely normal to be nervous about how they might react to sharing with a new little someone who needs even more of your attention and time.

Make sure to carve out some one-on-one time just for your little ones in the upcoming weeks. Tell them how special they are to you, and that they're going to have an important new job in the family as big brother or big sister—you're counting on them to help show their new sibling the ropes!

The new baby should always be presented as something exciting and wonderful for everyone to experience—if your older children don't seem scared or upset, *don't* tell them they should be! If they do express concerns and worries, ask them about why they're worried—and really *listen*. Maybe they're worried that the new baby will take their teddy bear or that you won't have time to read them bedtime stories anymore. Once you know your children's specific worries, you'll be able to calm them with answers, or explain what things might really be like after the baby arrives. Most of all, make sure your children feel *involved*. Taking them on a mini field trip to the hospital to show them where Mommy's going when the baby comes will help them understand that you're not gone forever when you're away from home, and it will make them feel like a vital part of your team—which of course they are!

Another good idea is to get your children started on a fun (and distracting!) new project in the weeks before the new baby comes. It will give them something to focus on and feel pride in while you're finding your groove with the new babe. None of this, of course, can totally erase the chance of a rough adjustment period, but it can surely make it easier.

Before and after the baby comes, grandparents can be amazing at helping your older children feel better. Try to ask that visits not be all about the newest member of the family—and keep a few small gifts on hand so that when people give presents to the baby, you have some for your older loves, too.

Four-legged family members

If you've got furry friends in the house, think about how they react to new people and situations. All of the commotion from a little one in the house can be upsetting to pets, and the sooner you help them find a safe space to retreat to when things get a little nutso, the happier everybody will be. Try moving food dishes and comfort toys to quieter areas of the house, away from where the baby will be spending most of his or her time. This will give your loyal Lab or curious kitty a sanctuary away from it all until he or she gets used to the newest member of the family.

It's also good to get your four-legged friend used to any baby-related sounds ahead of time so it isn't frightened or put on the defensive when they occur. Let your pet hear recordings of babies crying, put the swing into motion, and play that cute little music box you got for the crib. Really, the fewer surprises you can give your pet, the better off everyone will be.

Introduce baby toys to your dog or cat so it knows what they are and isn't frightened by them, but also teach your pet that those toys are different from its own, and that they're off-limits. Establishing (and enforcing!) these kinds of rules now can help prevent a lot of headaches later on.

And of course it's easy to paint your pet in the best light possible, but it's important to be honest with yourself here: Is Max a little aggressive? Does Sheba have a tendency to swipe? If either is true (or both!), call your local obedience school for advice. Chances are you'll be able to find a class that can help your animal friend chill out and welcome your little one with purrs, not paws!

Your fabulous friends

Most of us have been on the other end of this: you're having this exciting, childless life, and then Bingo!—one of your closest girlfriends has a baby and suddenly has no time to catch up. And then when she does have time for you, it's like all she can talk about is "diaper" this and "so cute!" that. "Oh, what, you got a new job? That's nice, let's keep talking about the baby." Even the most amazing friendships can grow lukewarm when a wee one arrives, but that does *not* have to happen to you.

Unless your friends are super into babies and have independently (no nudging from you!) expressed interest in helping out during the first few weeks, be upfront with them and let them know you might not be available for in-person meetings for about a month after you've had the baby—then plan a date to meet up for right after that time. Show them they're a priority, but that you also don't want to overpromise your time or guilt them into helping out with a newborn when it's just not their thing. They'll be thankful for your honesty!

And for Pete's sake, don't be selfish about the time you *do* have with your friends before or after the little one arrives. Of course you're all wrapped up in babyland, and they're probably interested, but chances are that's not *all* they want to talk about—so make sure to ask about their lives, their jobs, their partners, and even what they thought about *SNL* last night.

Yes, your friendships will change once the baby comes, but if you keep these things in mind your friendships may actually change for the better and deepen over time. As we support each other on our different paths, we become smarter, more interesting—dare I say more *lovable*—people. Continue being there for your friends, and they'll almost definitely return the favor.

Finding a pediatrician

If you don't already have a pediatrician for your little one, now's the time for a speedy search. Your baby needs to have his or her first appointment within the first week of birth, all being well and normal. If you wait to find a doctor, you'll end up scraping around at the last minute and you won't be able to make a choice based on the things that are truly important to you. You've been so careful about ensuring your baby has had the best from his or her first days in the womb, and clearly you want the best for baby's health out here in the big, germy world!

First, ask friends, coworkers, and family members you trust for pediatricians they'd recommend. Make a list of three to five names, and then start calling to arrange some face time with the doctors you're considering. Some docs have meet-and-greet times every few weeks for potential new patients, and others charge for a preliminary or "screening" appointment—but the fee is worth paying, since you want to make sure you and the doctor are on the same page.

Here are eight things to look for when interviewing potential pediatricians:

- ☑ The office is close to your home—you may need to get there quickly.

- ☑ The office has well and sick hours, so your healthy baby doesn't have to be exposed to potentially contagious kids during checkups.

- ☑ Does the doctor take patients who haven't had their vaccines on schedule? Is that okay with you?

- ☑ You have similar health and wellness philosophies.

- ☑ You *like* the doctor!

- ☑ The doctor or staff is available via email or to return phone messages between appointments—you'll probably have questions!

- ☑ The doctor is on time to your appointment and has a reputation for running a fairly on-time office.

- ☑ You feel like you can ask questions—no matter how simple or complicated—without being judged or treated with condescension. You shouldn't be expected to be an expert; that's the doctor's job!

You'll really know if a doctor is a good fit for you once you start going to appointments. Pediatricians are huge in the first year of your baby's life. They'll help with figuring out when and how much feeding should be done, establishing normal(ish!) naptimes, and so much more. Because of that, it's so important that you feel you're getting the best information from your doctor and that you feel absolutely comfortable asking questions. If something seems off or you're not totally into the doctor you've chosen, don't feel defeated, just start looking for a new pediatrician. There are plenty of great ones out there!

Wrapping up at work

If you're planning to take maternity leave, your 9-to-5 is about to wind down so you can get ready for a whole different, *round-the-clock* schedule. If you're getting paid or unpaid time off for your pregnancy, check in with HR to make sure you've provided them with any paperwork required and that you're both agreed on the dates you'll be out. Scan copies of any relevant paperwork and email them to yourself. With all the hubbub at the hospital on the big day, and at home in the weeks to come, you'll be glad you kept track of exactly when you're supposed to show up at the office again!

Also, make sure you know the process of adding your wee one to your health insurance. Some policies require notification within the first day or two of the baby's birth—and you want to make sure your son or daughter has the best care available from the start. Your HR person can tell you what you'll need to do. This is also a great job to give to your partner or a family member so you don't have to worry about it while you're at the hospital. And if you're worried about putting something so important in someone else's hands, just ask that person to tell you when it's all settled so you don't fret over whether or not it got done!

As for the actual *work* you do at work, make sure you finish up any projects you can, and then sit down with your boss to discuss a plan to delegate the work that will need to be done while you're out to other people in your office. Worried that it won't get done, and feeling bad about dumping so much on your (already hardworking) coworkers? Have cookies delivered to your office while you're away, and include a card thanking your colleagues for stepping up so you could step out with your baby. A little thoughtfulness can go a *long* way.

Early contractions—nothing to sneeze at!

You may have heard of "false" or Braxton Hicks contractions and think that any early contraction or cramping feeling you have around this time is nothing to worry about. Not true— if you're having those feelings right now, or anytime before week 37, which is about the middle of month nine, you *must* call your doctor. Early contractions at this stage could be a sign of preterm labor, and since more than one in 10 American babies is born premature, you can't assume this won't happen to yours.

Other signs of premature labor to look for before week 37 include a change in vaginal discharge, pelvic or abdominal pressure, vaginal bleeding, severe lower back pain, ongoing cramps like you're on your period, or rhythmic cramping pain. If you experience any of these, even if you think it might be nothing, get on that phone!

PAGING DR. GRUNEBAUM

What if I am going into preterm labor? Does that mean my baby will be premature? Will he or she have health problems?

Preterm labor is labor that happens before 37 weeks, or more than three weeks before your due date. If you call your doctor immediately upon having symptoms of premature labor, and can get to the hospital before going into labor, in some cases it's possible for him or her to give you medication that can actually stall labor so your child is not born prematurely. There is also an injection that can be administered before you go into preterm labor that goes to your baby to help prevent health issues associated with premature births, such as trouble breathing or brain bleeding—but that must be given 12 to 24 hours before the baby is born, so it's of the *utmost* importance to make the phone call if you suspect anything might be happening.

The health problems that your child might face due to a premature birth vary depending on how far along your pregnancy was at the time of delivery. If you deliver before 32 weeks, there is a much higher chance that the baby will not be able to breathe independently and will have a much more difficult time surviving outside the womb. Between 32 and 37 weeks, health problems can still arise, but they are more likely to be treatable, and depend on any complications that may have come up in your birth. No two premature babies are the same, but they are all at risk for complications.

The key is to alert your doctor to anything you think might be a sign of premature labor as soon as possible so you and your baby can get the best care.

Birth announcements

Okay, so the baby isn't really here yet, but once he or she is, you won't exactly be swimming in free time. If you don't get them ready now, those adorable birth announcements you've been planning on sending will likely gather dust for *months* before they even get stamps on them.

I always find the thing that takes the most time isn't picking out the design—it's

SMART BITS

Okay, you already know I'm a firm believer in the mantra that the better you look, the better you feel, no matter how tired, gigantic, or just plain *done* you might be feeling right now. My recommendation is to make sure you have something to wear after the baby gets here. We've all heard stories of celebs who went from pregnant to petite practically overnight—but unless you've got a dedicated trainer, a nanny to watch your baby, a cook, and a *whole* lot of time on your hands, that's probably not going to be you. In fact, some women can look like they're about five months pregnant for the first two months after giving birth, while other mothers slim down a lot quicker. Whichever camp you're in, some of the maternity outfits you've been rocking so far—tight around the belly with ruching detail up the sides—might look a little . . . deflated on your post-baby body.

Pop online or hop out for a quick shopping trip and get a few new things for after the baby's here—you're going to be photographed a ton, and you want to be wearing something that you feel cuter and more confident in than your partner's old college sweatshirt!

Something wonderful to add to your wardrobe right now? A few pretty ivory or cream-colored tops. I know, you're thinking, "How impractical can this lady get? Cream when a baby's on the way—that'll show every little dribble!" I thought the same thing, too, until I realized (the hard way!) that baby spit-up shows up and stays on dark-colored clothing but blends right in with creamy vanilla hues. So go light—it will help keep you looking clean and maybe even brighten your mood a little in the process, too!

addressing all those pesky envelopes! Do yourself this major favor while you can: invite a friend or two over, whip up a batch of mocktails, and crank out those addresses together while you've got the luxury of time. Let's face it, we all wish we could spend more time with our favorite ladies, and this is a perfect way to do that while also check-ing off a major "to-do" from your list. Multitasking? A mommy's biggest talent.

The main point is to not let perfection get in the way of intention. You may want the announcements to all be addressed in gorgeous hand-drawn calligraphy, but if you don't have time for that (and who realistically does?), just get them done however you can. You'll be so glad when they're checked off your list!

And if you think you'll want to email photos of your little one on the big day, now's a good time to make sure you have all those contacts handy and in order. Can you imagine how upset your dear cousin Bertha would be if she was the only one who didn't get a picture? I rest my case.

Strategy check-in

Seriously, how are you really feeling about the big day? It's coming up so quickly, and I want you to feel the most confident that you can when your little one makes his or her big debut. To have that level of self-assurance, it's important to revisit that birth strategy you and your partner came up with months ago and make sure it's still the most comfortable fit. Also, definitely revisit it with your doctor and make sure he or she agrees it's still practical for you. As your pregnancy has progressed, certain issues or complications may have made your strategy no longer ideal for your situation, and it's better to know that kind of thing in advance!

I know, you've already been through this—you've thought about who you want delivering your baby (in an ideal situation), where you want the birth to happen, and whether or not you'd like the help of pain management drugs. But every great lady (and *you're* one of them, sweets!) is allowed to change her mind, and over the months you may have learned a little more or realized your preferences aren't what you thought they'd be at the start.

Even if you're pretty sure you won't want medicinal help to dull the pain on baby's big day, it's helpful to know your options just in case you change your mind in the delivery room. The three kinds of pain relief assistance you'll hear about being used during labor include an epidural, Demerol, and tranquilizers. It's good to talk to your doctor about what he or she uses most. I'm not saying you'll need prescription help in the pain department, but it is *always* good to be informed and know your options. Knowledge leads to confidence, and confidence leads to great mothering!

PAGING DR. GRUNEBAUM

What are the pros and cons of an epidural, Demerol, and tranquilizers? I want to make the best choice if I decide to go with a pain intervention.

I always say that it's your pain and your delivery, so nobody should talk you *into* or *out of* a pain management intervention—but if you are planning on using one or if you realize during labor that you would like to have some help dealing with the discomfort, you'll find that most doctors agree with me in preferring an epidural to anything else.

Epidurals—both the combined spinal epidural, in which a small amount of a narcotic and an anesthetic are administered, and the "walking" epidural, in which only the anesthetic is administered—are very safe these days if given by an experienced anesthesiologist. There are of course risks with any medical intervention, and although the chances of these risks occurring are few and far between, it is worth mentioning them. Some women experience more numbness than intended to the degree where she cannot move her legs, while other women do not feel enough numbness. Occasionally, the baby's heart rate may be affected, but that can be managed relatively easily with other medication. It's very uncommon for a mother to get an infection due to an epidural; it will not affect your brain, so you can be alert and engaged while your child is being brought into this world; and in the vast majority of cases, it numbs you from the waist down, relieving a lot of discomfort. A small percentage (fewer than 5 percent) of women experience what is called a "spinal headache" a few days after having the combined spinal epidural, but once brought to a doctor's attention, that can be remedied through a very simple procedure. Like any medical intervention, the epidural does not have a 100 percent guaranteed success rate—but for many women, its benefits outweigh the potential side effects.

Demerol is not nearly as safe. It affects your brain, so you're not as alert, and also affects your natural reflexes. That means if you throw up, which is not uncommon in childbirth, you're much more likely to aspirate and choke, which can be very serious. Moreover, it can negatively affect the baby's heartbeat. I would not recommend Demerol, especially in any situation where an epidural is available.

Finally, and I cannot stress this enough, tranquilizers should *never* be given during childbirth. When they spread through your body, they cross the placenta, which means they go right into your baby as well as yourself. These kinds of heavy drugs are severely dangerous for newborns and can lead to devastating impairments.

Who's in your tribe?

You've already got:

- ○ Your partner and/or your best friend

- ○ Your doctor or midwife

- ○ Your parents and in-laws

- ○ A mommy workout buddy

- ○ An all-star event planner

- ○ Your birth and parenting teachers

- ○ You (you're the most important member, silly!)

And you're adding:

- ○ Your group of close friends—whether or not they're experienced with motherhood, they all have pretty good penmanship and can help you knock out those announcements (and keep you distracted with fun and gossip while you wait for the big day!)

Murmurs from the Man Cave

Here you are, just weeks away from giving birth, all consumed by how it will happen. You want everything to be perfect for you, your baby, and your partner—but does he really care whether you use an epidural or have a small orchestra in the room to play Brahms as the baby arrives? I snuck into the Man Cave to find out, and you might be pleasantly surprised by what I discovered.

How much did you care about the birth strategy—such as where she'd give birth, what kind of doctor or midwife she'd have, and whether she'd use pain interventions? Were you involved? Did you have strong opinions?

"That stuff was all up to her. She was the one having to give birth, so whatever she wanted (within reason!) was fine with me."

"That did *not* matter to me."

"She wanted a doula, and I didn't want to pay for it, since our insurance wouldn't cover it. I'm glad I gave in, though—it was the best money I ever spent, because it made the delivery so much easier for both of us."

The takeaway

Chances are, beyond the cost of things (which we already know is on his mind!), your partner doesn't care about much in the delivery room besides you and your baby staying healthy. So if something doesn't go according to plan, or you have second thoughts about using a pain intervention, don't feel like you're letting him down. He just wants you to get through this and to get that baby, no matter how it has to happen.

Month Nine

the final countdown

Mommy IQ:

What you'll be figuring out this month

- ○ Baby's achievements

- ○ Braxton Hicks—he's that new country star, right?

- ○ Am I going into labor?

- ○ Getting a jump start (if you need it)

- ○ Dealing with great expectations

- ○ The photos you *don't* want on Facebook

- ○ What's in your bag?

- ○ Your post-delivery survival kit

- ○ In case you're terrified of delivery

- ○ Who's in your tribe?

- ○ Murmurs from the Man Cave

{ My **Mommy IQ** is ___ out of 11 }

My mind is *always* racing right before a baby comes—what if the car breaks down right as I'm going into labor and we have to take the subway, and then there's a problem with the subway and I have to give birth right there underground, just before appearing on the evening news?! The scenarios I come up with can be kind of . . . *imaginative,* to say the least.

But that inner dialogue is precisely why I always make myself take a window of quiet time in those last few weeks when I can really just sit back and think about the *awesomeness* of what is about to happen—a whole new person is about to live on this earth—and what's already happened—I've *made* that person inside of me!

Being a parent is a massive responsibility—I mean, you are going to play a huge part in shaping this amazing human being. Don't let other things get in the way of recognizing the importance of your role. When you're in the moment and your baby needs feeding and you haven't slept and you're still healing from the delivery, it can be hard to focus on the miracle of it all. So take time now to think about how privileged you are to be a mother, and how blessed your entire family will be by this birth.

I know it's hard to not worry, especially if you've heard a few war stories from deliveryland, but trust in your doctors, trust in your tribe to be there for you, and mainly, trust in yourself. You're a mother, and mothers are made of the strongest stuff out there: *love.*

Rosie's maternity mantras

That big red circle on your calendar is just days away, and whether you're a little freaked out (totally understandable!) or just beyond excited, there's no way to manipulate time and make the day come faster or slower. And I hate to say it, but there's also no way to guarantee that the day you've circled—your baby's due date—is actually going to be the big day. In fact, fewer than 5 percent of babies are born on the day doctors predict, with about half of the rest arriving just before and the other half just after! So unless you have a planned C-section, that little babe really could be coming any day now.

I can assure you, that day, whenever it does come, will be crazytunes. Not because anything will go wrong (it most likely won't), but because giving birth *changes you*. It makes you see the world in a totally different way, and gives you a new appreciation for the things that really matter. You can't ever fully prepare for that feeling, but you can prepare for the nitty-gritty details of what will go on around you in the delivery room. That tiny bit of extra prep will help you relax and really cherish the first moments with your babe—well worth it, in my book!

Here are a couple of little thoughts that might help get you through these final days and weeks of waiting.

> " We must be **willing to let go** of the life we have planned, so as to have the life that is **waiting for us**."
>
> —E. M. FORSTER, AUTHOR

> " If pregnancy were a book, they would **cut the last two chapters**."
>
> —NORA EPHRON, SCREENWRITER

Baby's achievements

That little baby inside you has made it to full term! I raise a mocktail to both of you! Even if you're hard on yourself some days, and even if you think you could have been a better protector of your wee one during these past months, you've succeeded in growing a baby who's ready to come out into this big, wide world. And that, my lovely, is *definitely* something to celebrate.

Last month, your babe topped out at around 20 inches—remember, roughly the size of a pair of tall boots? Well, he or she isn't stretching out any more (and thank goodness for that; I'm not sure if your belly could handle it!), but more and more cuddly fat is being added to those cute little arms and legs so your sweetie will be ready for snuggles with Mommy in just a few days or weeks. (That weight on the scale isn't all *you* after all!)

Although this isn't a new trick, your wee one is sucking on his or her thumb more and more as practice for breast or bottle feeding. He or she still might not be perfect at latching on to your jubblies after this in-womb training, but at least seeds of the general idea have been planted.

Finally, in preparation for all those adorable little onesies you've picked out for your baby's first weeks, your little one has shed most of the petroleum-like coating and fuzzy outer layer on his or her skin—leaving those oh-so-touchable fingers and toes and that round little tummy ready to be adored.

Braxton Hicks—he's that new country star, right?

Some might think Braxton Hicks contractions—those uncomfortable, squeezing sensations any of you might be feeling in your uterus this month—are happening just to torture you. The truth, of course, is that Braxton Hicks contractions are actually helping to prepare your muscles (and your natural pain management system) for the *real* contractions you'll be feeling before and during labor.

Even though most Braxton Hicks contractions last for less than a minute, some can go longer, making you feel tense for a couple of minutes or more at a time—especially as you get close to the big day. Dehydration can make you more likely to have these contractions, so if you want to keep them to a minimum, make sure you're getting plenty of water and fluids throughout the day.

If Braxton Hicks have got you feeling beat, try doing the exact opposite of what you were doing when they came on. If you were walking with friends, sit or lie down for a minute. If you were lounging on the couch, go for a little walk. If switching up your activity doesn't help—if the squeezing feeling gets stronger, or if you're having more than four of these contractions within an hour—you really could be in labor. Get on the phone and tell your doc exactly what's going on, lady! This could be the big day!

PAGING DR. GRUNEBAUM

What if I don't feel any of these Braxton Hicks contractions? Is there something wrong?

I don't like the term "Braxton Hicks" contractions, because all contractions— even if they turn out to be false—should be paid attention to, and many women just brush them off assuming they're false when they're not. If you're experiencing anything that you think might be labor, call your doctor! That said, not every woman will experience them, and that's fine and normal.

Am I going into labor?

From the movies and TV, you'd think that *every* woman went through pre-labor teasers, like mini-announcements that their bodies were almost ready to deliver—but that's *so* not true. I kept waiting and waiting for my water to break, but eventually it was sort of "broken" for me at the hospital!

With that in mind, and with the knowledge that each one of us is built differently and goes through a unique experience in pregnancy, here are the little flags your body might (or might not!) wave to let you know the time is getting close:

You're uncorked!

If you see a strange-looking, clearish blobby bit that's maybe a little blood-tinged in the toilet after you've done your business, chances are that's the mucus plug that has been sealing off your cervix during your pregnancy. It's pretty common for it to become dislodged and leave your body in the weeks before your baby arrives, but some women don't notice it or even lose it until the very end. No biggie either way.

What's that pinky schmear?

If there's a bit of pinkish discharge in your undies or when you wipe, don't freak. It's normal for blood vessels in your cervix to burst as you dilate, and when that teeny bit of blood mixes with your regular discharge, *voilà*—it's pink! Again, this might not happen to you, but it's good to know about just in case, and of course you should let your doctor know about it so he or she knows what to expect in the upcoming weeks. That said, if your discharge is bright, stop-sign red, call your doctor *immediately*. You could be having a medical emergency and need attention right away.

Waterworks

As I mentioned, not all women will have their water break, but it is the most classic indication that you're just hours away from contractions. If you notice fluid and aren't sure if it's a bit of wee (I know, bladder control is sometimes kind of out the window at this point!), or your water breaking, take a little sniff. If it's sweet-smelling, that's from the baby, and a sure sign that you're not far away from the big moment. If it's kind of acidic, and smelling like . . . wee, then that's probably what it is! Oh, and as for that Niagara Falls of water gushing down between women's legs that you see in movies and on TV? That's a *bit* of an exaggeration. For some women, it's nothing more than a trickle. All kidding aside, though, if your water breaks, call your doctor. If your water breaks and the fluid is brown or dark in color, call your doctor *right away*—even if it's off hours or the middle of the night. This could be a sign that you and your baby need extra care.

Contractions

Here . . . we . . . go! You can start to feel contractions (really intense cramps rolling and tightening through your belly area) and not have to go to the doctor right away. Luckily for you, there's a thing called 5-1-1. 5-1-1 is a handy way of remembering that when your contractions have been five minutes (or less) apart, lasting for about one minute each, and happening for one hour, it's time to call the doc. When my contractions started in my first pregnancy, it was the weekend, so when I called, I got Dr. Grunebaum's answering service. They offered to page him if it was an emergency, and I said no, don't bother. My husband asked what happened, said, "Um, honey, this is an emergency! You're going into labor!" and made me call back. Just hearing my doctor's voice on the other end of the line made me feel so much better. My point? You don't have to go through this on your own. There's a professional on your side, and now is the time to make good use of that professional's expertise.

I don't want to bother my doctor or to seem alarmist—when should I really call my doctor?

If your contractions are following the 5-1-1 pattern, get on the phone! But seriously, call your doctor *anytime* you're concerned about an issue—especially as you get closer to the delivery date. Some of the issues you absolutely must call about include vaginal bleeding, abdominal pain or cramping, severe headache, breathing problems or chest pain. And *of course* when you think your water has broken, you feel increased pelvic pressure, or there's a change in fetal movements such as more or less than usual. We will never think you're crazy or paranoid—more that you are being a wonderful mother and looking out for your child already.

Getting a jump start (if you need it)

Sometimes, even in totally healthy, complication-free pregnancies, labor just doesn't start when your doctor thinks it should. Maybe your water broke, but labor doesn't start quickly enough. Or perhaps your baby becomes officially overdue around the 42-week mark. Whatever the reasons, if your doctor thinks it's best to induce labor, there's really nothing to worry about. I just think it's best for you to know what might happen ahead of time, just in case this happens to you. There's also, of course, nothing to feel bad about. Pregnancies, as you know, are all different, and it's impossible to predict how any one of them will go. Just try to relax and be excited that your little one is coming soon.

If your doctor feels that you need a bit of assistance to go into labor, he or she may have you come into the office. There, the doctor can "strip the membrane," which separates the amniotic sac from the bottom of your uterus. This outpatient procedure might be uncomfortable (your doctor's hand is up there!), but it's not usually painful and you can almost always go home afterward.

If that didn't work to get things going, your doctor may soften your cervix with a vaginal gel or suppository, which is usually done in the hospital. It's not a difficult process and often helps labor come more quickly. Finally, if contractions still aren't starting, your doctor might give you Pitocin, which is a synthetic form of oxytocin, a hormone women's bodies typically produce during childbirth. The Pitocin can kick-start your contractions, and your doctor will probably give you a steady stream of it until those contractions start and keep happening regularly. Once you've been given Pitocin, you will stay in the hospital until the baby is born.

If none of that gets you going, you might be a candidate for a C-section, which we'll talk about more in the next chapter. Read ahead on pages 202–4 if you want to know more about that now.

PAGING DR. GRUNEBAUM

I've heard that Pitocin is controversial, because of something to do with bonding with the baby. What's the deal with it, and should I be worried?

Pitocin, a synthesized version of oxytocin, was first made over 50 years ago, and the doctor who created it won the Nobel Prize! It's still the number-one drug used in labor and delivery, since it's not only given sometimes to urge labor on, but also given after delivery to help prevent hemorrhage—the leading cause of death in childbirth. In that capacity, Pitocin has saved many, *many* women's lives over decades since it was introduced.

Pitocin can also be given to induce or stimulate labor when contractions are not as frequent or strong as desired. Many critics have concerns that it's being used too frequently for those purposes, and those critics are probably correct! Using oxytocin incorrectly can lead to a woman having too many contractions or an abnormal heart rate in the baby, and it can increase the C-section rate.

Therefore, you need to understand under what conditions your doctor is recommending Pitocin. Pitocin should be administered to induce labor (at a slow rate) only when the baby's heart rate is stable and you are having no more than five contractions in 10 minutes on average.

Some women say the contractions experienced after a dose of Pitocin are much more intense and painful than those they've had without it, but it is still up to you whether or not you want a pain intervention. No one should tell you that you should or should not have an epidural if you are being given Pitocin (or at any other point!). This is still your pregnancy, and it is still your choice.

As for whether or not Pitocin decreases the ability to bond right away with your baby, that is still up in the air, and many studies are being done on it. But either way, if Pitocin is necessary for you to safely deliver your baby, I think that would take precedence over how easily you'll bond any day.

Dealing with great expectations

By now, you've revisited your birth strategy about 20 bazillion times and know just how you want everything to go. Still, no matter how much you hope for all to be perfect, sometimes things beyond your control happen—and sometimes you just change your mind when you're going through something as intense as childbirth.

Maybe you don't think you'll want any medical interventions to deal with the pain of labor, but then halfway through decide that an epidural would be best. Whatever happens, the important thing is to not be hard on yourself, and to really try to not feel disappointed or like you're letting someone down when things don't go exactly as planned.

The most important thing is that you end up holding your gorgeous, healthy little baby, and that you have a whole future to grow and learn about each other. Those first few moments of discovery—what do his or her eyes look like? Look at those tiny little toes!—are so wonderful and full of complete joy, it would be a shame to cloud them with disappointment or guilt. So let those expectations and bits of self-doubt fly out the window when they need to, and just accept where the ride takes you.

The photos you *don't* want on Facebook

We've all seen them—pics of our model-gorgeous friends just after birth, hair a mess, sweaty, with their jubblies practically spilling out of their falling-off hospital gown. And if you're like me, you think, "The baby is darling, but I *know* she didn't okay that pic before it went up!"

If you don't want the whole wide world to see what you *really* looked like during, and just after, the big moment, talk to your partner now and give him a few photo guidelines. I learned this the hard way: After my first son was born, my husband emailed a photo of me—with a very-near hospital gown peep show going on!—to all my coworkers and friends. I nearly died, which is why before my next pregnancy we set ground rules that photos going out without my approval could *only* be of the baby (not me!) and that if he wanted to send snaps of me, too, he'd need to show them to me first.

We haven't had another slipped-gown slip-up since then, and I hope that *you* won't have to un-tag yourself from any unflattering photos once you have this little talk with the people who'll be in your delivery room!

What's in your bag?

Your hospital bag is like no overnight bag you've packed before, or will ever pack again (until you have another baby, that is!). Heaven knows it took me three pregnancies to finally get it right—remember the crime novels I took along to my first child's birth? Not exactly worth the space they took up. And contrary to my previous delusional beliefs, no new mommy walks out of the hospital in her pre-pregnancy skinny jeans—so let's just nix them from the list right from the get-go!

What you *do* need are a whole lot of pretty practical, and sometimes surprising, things. If my suggestions don't make a lot of sense right now, trust me that they will once the baby has arrived:

1. Lip balm: It sounds random, but your lips can actually get very dry during delivery, and there is nothing more annoying than cracked or even bleeding lips when you are trying to focus on getting through a contraction.

2. Hair ties: Even though you may arrive at the hospital looking like Lady Lovely Locks, you will soon want all the fuss and muss swept away from your face.

3. Snacky bits: You won't be able to eat during labor but your partner will probably be starving, especially if it's a long delivery (and believe me when I say you'll need his support and energy!). Also, after you've had your baby you will probably be hungrier than you've ever been, and for reasons I still cannot understand, you'll never be able to find anything scrumptious at the hospital. Come prepared.

4. Delivery menus: If you live in a city where delivery is the norm (hey there, NYC girls!), bring a few menus with you to the hospital. I can't tell you how nice it was to order in our favorite Italian dish after each of our children was born. The questionable fish that was offered at hospital mealtime didn't hold a candle. Besides, *no one* wants to eat fish after she's given birth—I don't care how much you love it!

5. Comfy but cute clothes: Think of a few outfits that won't make you feel self-conscious about your belly. You will probably look as though you are about five months pregnant for the first few days after delivery, so bring clothes that you feel good in and that don't accentuate the belly. The hospital is no place to worry about getting back into shape! Anything that opens in the front is going to make breastfeeding a whole lot easier, and remember that you want to like these outfits and feel like you look good in them, because a ton of pictures will be snapped in those first few days with the baby. Cozy silk jammies with button fronts are great (buttons make it easy for nursing), but yoga-type outfits with cozy wrapped cardigans are my absolute favorite (especially since most hospitals tend to be quite chilly—*brrr!*).

6. Two nursing bras and a breastfeeding pillow: These are bulky, but you'll be glad you've got them. Just trust me on that.

7. Flip-flops: You'll be schlepping a bit around the hospital, and you want easy-on, easy-off shoes that you'll feel okay wearing in the shower, too. Going barefoot in a common-use shower can be a bit icky.

8. Mini grooming kit for you and your baby: This should have your moisturizer, makeup, makeup remover, hair care products, body wash, toothbrush and toothpaste, and a mini nail file for your baby. (Many babies are born with long, rough nails, and you'll want to file them down so they don't scratch that pretty little face!)

9. A bunch of undies you don't mind throwing out: No need to go into too much detail here, but you will likely bleed a bit after delivery, and the disposable underwear provided by the hospital can be a bit flimsy. Popping a pack or two of simple cotton panties (maybe seven or eight pair total) into your bag is a good idea. If you are going to have a C-section or think you might, make sure they are extra low-rise so they sit under, instead of on top of, your scar.

10. Adult undergarments: These aren't glamorous, and you don't have to advertise that you're packing them, but you'll probably need them, so it's good to be prepared. Let's just say that when you have visitors, it can be hard to get to the bathroom in time, and these will become your BFFs.

11. Contact list: Whom do you want to text or email once the baby is born? Make sure you and your partner both have that list handy so you don't forget anybody.

12. Cell phone charger: Nightmare scenario: You're all ready to call your loved ones and tell them the big news when you notice your phone has pooped out. Luckily, since you thought ahead, you can just plug it right in and be good-to-go.

13. Note pad and a pen: You might want to jot down important information that they tell you at the hospital. Or you may just want to write a few thoughts once you have met your baby. It is truly one of the most amazing times in a person's life but it can often be a bit of a haze, so don't be afraid to write things down—from feelings and thoughts, to how many feedings you've done and when, to questions you want to ask the doctor or nurses when they come on their rounds.

14. Your lactation consultant's info: If you plan on nursing, you'll be so glad to have this. Many hospitals will provide lactation consultants upon request, but they have lots of people to see and often can't spend enough time with you. If you have any problems or concerns—even if they seem like no big deal—call the lactation consultant and have her come to the hospital or meet you when you get home. It is better to fix any problems before they get out of hand.

15. Going-home outfits for the baby and for you: The hospital will probably dress your baby in a little kimono, hat, and swaddle blanket. I suggest bringing socks, a blanket, and two outfits you've picked out for the baby. Remember, though, that the clothes should be kitten-soft, comfortable, and not complicated. I know you probably have the urge to dress your baby in a cute three-piece suit, but you and baby will be much happier with onesies and kimono sets while his or her belly button heals.

What about diapers, wipes, the bassinet, and everything else? No need to bring those, because the hospital will provide it all for you. And remember that your partner or a member of your tribe can always go home and grab whatever you forgot. As long as you and your new family are together enjoying the first very special moments as a unit, everything is just the way it was supposed to be.

Your post-delivery survival kit

Yes, that's right—you don't just need to pack for the hospital, you also have to prepare a few things for the days following the big homecoming. I used to think this was silly (I have everything I need at home already, *don't I?*) until after my first son was born. It was only then that I wished I'd done a teeny bit of extra preparation. Here's the short list of things you'll be so happy to have on hand during those first few days and weeks:

1. Delivery menus and frozen meals: You'll have to keep your energy up, and you won't have the time (or the strength, likely!) to stand at the stove to whip up your famous lasagna after fussing over baby all day and night. Do yourself a huge favor and cook a few things that freeze well now, or if you're not exactly Julia Child (I'm not!), just stock up on reliable delivery menus or some premade frozen stuff. Mommies need to eat!

2. Tons of clean sheets, towels, and basics: You're not exactly going to be up to doing laundry, either, and having a stockpile of fresh basics on hand will be super comforting. If you're not ready to do laundry once that stockpile is depleted, take it all to the wash-and-fold and let *them* do the work. It's worth spending an extra couple of bucks to have everything nice and ready for your first few days of mommyhood.

3. Mommy-friendly outfits: Remember those ivory tops I suggested you get a couple of months ago? Well, you're going to want them when the baby (and his or her spit-up!) is here. Basically, it's just a smart idea to have five or six full outfits already put together and ready to pop on in the days after you come home from the hospital. You won't have the energy to think about what you're wearing, and if you don't plan your clothes in advance, you'll likely be in old, ratty sweats for weeks. Repeat after me: when you look good, you feel better, and when you feel better, you can be a better mom. I really believe this, and in the days after giving birth, you may need this trick more than ever!

4. The phone number of your lactation consultant: I know this was in your hospital bag, too, but if you're breastfeeding, I can't stress enough how helpful this will be. Call her, and call her often if needed. You'll feel so much more confident with her on your side.

5. More adult diapers: There's a bit of leaking down there in the days after you give birth, and you'll be happy to know you're fully covered just in case.

6. A doughnut to sit on: If you're experiencing postnatal hemorrhoids or had an episiotomy, this will definitely make your first few days a bit easier and more comfortable!

In case you're terrified of delivery

For some women, there's absolutely no fear surrounding delivery. It's a calm process and their bodies just know what they're supposed to do. It's amazing. But if you're one of those women who feel woozy at even the *thought* of contractions, you're not alone. So many women tell these war stories and make giving birth seem like something out of a sci-fi horror movie (and you might, too, when all is said and done!), but it's not like that when you're actually going through it.

Sure, it's not easy, and there's blood involved, but when you're focused on getting this miracle of life to emerge from your body, you're not focused on *any of that*. The gore, the pain? All of that goes out the window, and the only thing you care about is helping your baby make a healthy entrance into this world.

The best thing I think you can do to help yourself in this situation is to talk to your doctor about just how scared you are, and why. There's no need to put on a brave face—and besides, communication like this will help your doctor keep you calm during the parts that worry you the most.

PAGING DR. GRUNEBAUM

I know I'm supposed to be excited, but really, I'm terrified of giving birth. What can I do?

The best thing you can do at this point is to tell your doctor about your concerns. He or she can help walk you through any part of the delivery process you're worried about, can introduce you to the anesthesiologist and other members of the team, and can set you up with a hospital tour if you haven't taken one yet. Sometimes just having someone else know how frightened you are can calm your fears.

Who's in your tribe?

You've already got:

- ○ Your partner and/or your best friend

- ○ Your doctor or midwife

- ○ Your parents and in-laws

- ○ A mommy workout buddy

- ○ An all-star event planner

- ○ Your birth and parenting teachers

- ○ You (you're the most important member, silly!)

- ○ Your group of close friends

And you're adding:

- ○ Your lactation consultant if you're breastfeeding

- ○ The delivery guy at your favorite takeout spot (you'll get to know him well!)

Murmurs from the Man Cave

You think your mind is racing? So is your partner's. Don't believe me? Come with me as I spy on the guys in the Man Cave.

As the big day got closer, what was on your mind?

"I couldn't shake how much our lives were going to change. We were used to going out to dinner and seeing live music whenever we wanted. All of that was going to change literally overnight."

"I was really just ready for it to all happen. I don't think I had any idea how much things were going to change."

"I was so ready to be a dad. I couldn't wait."

The takeaway

You might be feeling nervous, excited, and even apprehensive about that little baby's arrival, but so is your partner! Don't clam up about your feelings. Talk about them together, and chances are you'll both feel a little better in the process. These big changes you're about to go through will affect both of you, and it's important to discuss them head-on *before* the baby gets here.

The Big Day

(but *don't* wait until the big day to read this—please read ahead!)

Mommy IQ:

What you'll be figuring out this month

- ○ When to go to the hospital

- ○ The truth about episiotomies

- ○ If you're getting an epidural

- ○ Food might not be your friend (but it is for your partner)

- ○ C-section survival

- ○ Having a baby, step-by-step

- ○ 10 gross things nobody will notice (and you probably don't want to share)

- ○ Baby mine (or, um, yours!)

- ○ Who's in your tribe?

- ○ Murmurs from the Man Cave

{ My **Mommy IQ** is ___ out of 10 }

Whether this baby is your first, your 15th (you deserve a medal!), or somewhere in-between, the day you give birth to this little angel is going to be one of the most important and meaningful experiences of your life. You'll not only see the very sweet fruit of your labor, but you'll also see a *future*—full of love and kisses, first tricycles and skinned knees, puppy love and college applications—all laid out before you in one lovely, space-efficient bundle. It's overwhelmingly wonderful and not something you'll ever forget, but I do have a piece of advice for first-time mommies, based on my own experience.

When I had my first child, my husband was completely consumed with what was going on every second. He was holding my hand, telling me what an amazing job I was doing, and getting damp cloths for my forehead even when I didn't need them. I mean, I knew he was a good guy to begin with—I married him, didn't I?—but he was outstanding in that instance!

So, when I went into labor with my second child, I figured things would be pretty much the same. I'd do all the physical work, but my husband would be right there with me, waiting breathlessly from the minute we got to the hospital, on edge for baby's big debut. To my surprise, things *changed* a bit the second go-around. Yes, he was there, and yes, he was fantastic—especially near the end—but it was just . . . different. At one point before I went into heavy labor, I looked over and he was in the corner eating a chicken sandwich, checking the scores on the big game, and I knew the first-baby rush had gone out of him.

At first I wondered if he didn't care as much this time, but then near the end, when the baby was really coming, I saw my husband snap to attention—attending to my every need and asking the doctor what was happening at every turn.

I guess the thing is, he'd figured out that there can be a *lot* of time between getting to the hospital and having a baby, and that there's not always something huge going on at every moment. It wasn't that he cared even a drop less, it was more that he knew what to expect a little more so he could relax (and naturally, keep up with the game!).

So, my advice for first-timers? Bask in all the adulation and attention you'll be getting from your partner or whoever is there in the room with you—it might not be quite like this again! And for those of you who are going into labor for a second time or more, go easy on your partner if he takes a break or two to grab a snack or call a friend. It's a big day for him, too, but when your partner is not directly—physically—involved, he just might need a few things to *do* until things get really active.

Now, take a deep breath, and know I'm thinking of you. You're going to be great—from start to finish, and for a long, sweet time after that!

Rosie's maternity mantras

Giving birth is one of those extremely personal moments in your life. You're about to meet the person who you're going to love more than anything in the world—but you have no idea what that person looks like, what he or she will be like. Meeting your baby is an amazing experience—it's something that you can't even imagine until you're holding that baby in your arms.

Every time I end up in the delivery room, I start anxiously telling my husband, "Today we're having a baby!" as if I can somehow mark the importance with words, but it's not about announcements and fanfare, it's about the experience itself. When you're in it, you're maybe even too in it to appreciate how amazing it is—but when you look back, as you will, you'll see just how miraculous this event was—what an absolute blessing your child is, and how happy you are to have gone through it all (even the rough bits!).

Childbirth isn't easy, and it's not all pretty—but it is *beautiful* in a greater way than I may be able to express here. So, hold on tight, and get ready to meet your baby!

> " We have a **secret** in our culture: it's not that birth is painful, it's that *women* are strong. "
>
> —LAURA STAVOE HARM, AUTHOR

> " I'm not interested in being **Wonder Woman** in the delivery room. **Give me drugs.** "
>
> —MADONNA

When to go to the hospital

If you remember my story from the beginning of the book, about how I went to the hospital way too early to deliver my first son, you know I wasn't always an expert on this—but to be quite frank, who is? Excitement gets in the way, and every delivery is different, so don't be hard on yourself if you're not sure how you'll know the time is right. After adding two more sweet little ones to my family, I'd like to think I've gotten the hang of it, but every pregnancy is different, and somehow between births I've experienced mommy amnesia! Every time I approach the big day, I second-guess myself. That's why I'm handing you over to the wonderful Dr. G—he's the one I learned everything from, and I thought you should get the same info.

The truth about episiotomies

When I talk to women about giving birth the thing they ask about, and are more concerned about than anything else, is the episiotomy. As you've probably heard, an episiotomy is a cut that is sometimes made right before you deliver between the vaginal opening and the rectum that makes it easier for the baby to pass through. I know that the thought of anyone cutting you down there sounds . . . well, even less fun than a Brazilian wax gone wrong, so I thought knowing more about this procedure might make you feel a little better (and calmer, and less likely to run screaming from the hospital!). Here are three things I was very surprised to learn:

1. Episiotomies don't always happen, so you might not even have to have one.

2. If you have an epidural, you don't feel the procedure at all.

3. These things take time to heal, but then your body will be normal again. Promise!

So many women are terrified of this part of the birth, but trust me, it's the last thing you care about in the moment. Now, to explain it in a bit more scientific language, I'll make way for Dr. Grunebaum (who I'm sure you'd rather hear from on this anyway!).

PAGING DR. GRUNEBAUM

Will I have to have an episiotomy?

Probably not! Episiotomies used to be routine, but that practice has stopped, and now they are only given in certain circumstances—such as when the baby's head is particularly large, when the baby's heart rate is such that a quicker delivery is needed, or when a woman has been pushing for an extremely long period and delivery needs some assistance. All that said, today, 10 percent or fewer women in labor receive episiotomies.

If you're getting an epidural

Of course not every woman needs or wants medical pain intervention, but since six out of every 10 American women giving birth vaginally are aided by an epidural, I think it's worth exploring and explaining a bit. There's a lot of misconception about medical pain management (I was clueless before I met Dr. Grunebaum!), and I want you to have the all the info you can so you feel safe and confident in your decisions. I'm not saying you should our shouldn't have an epidural; what I am saying is that you should make an educated decision and not listen to every random story people want to offer. That's why Dr. Grunebaum is here to walk you through every step:

PAGING DR. GRUNEBAUM

How soon or how late can you wait to get an epidural if you decide at the last minute? Is there a point where it's too early or too late?

Yes, there is a too early and a too late: Too early is when you're still at home! Too late is after the baby is born. The anesthesiologist can administer the epidural as soon as you are admitted to your room and actually anytime up until it's obvious the baby is on its way and will be born in the next 15 minutes or less.

Depending on the hospital, how busy they are, and how many staff they have, it can take 20 to 40 minutes for the doctor and anesthesiologist to place an epidural. From the time it's given, it usually takes 10 minutes for pain relief to be significant enough to be noticeable. If you are considering an epidural, you should talk to your nurse or doctor about how long it will take in your instance.

I have no preference as to whether or not my patients have epidurals, because as I tell them and will tell you, it's your pain, not mine! Do not let anyone talk you in or out of it. In the end, it's you who will have to endure the pain, so it truly is your decision.

How is an epidural given?

The woman is usually sitting up when the epidural needle goes into a prenumbed area in the back near her spinal cord, and then before the needle is withdrawn, a small tube or catheter is usually left in that space, allowing for injections of medication to be given as needed.

Are there different kinds?

Yes, there are two different kinds. There is the traditional epidural as described above, and the "walking" epidural, which does not last as long, but which allows you to move more freely in the bed. You should speak to the anesthesiologist about which might be better for you.

I've heard that epidurals don't work perfectly for every woman, that they can make delivery take longer, and that they can cause the mother-to-be to have headaches. Is this true?

Epidurals are a lot like husbands. Not all husbands are going to be a good match for you, and not all husbands turn out to be good guys, but even knowing this, people still get married! Just like that, most epidurals are good, but they are not guaranteed to work 100 percent for every woman.

An epidural is a medical procedure. There is no medical procedure that always works and never has any complications. Some procedures have more complications than others, and some will produce more of a benefit. It is rare, but sometimes a doctor will have to place a second epidural because the first one didn't work. Rarer still are complications such as bleeding at the site or infection. That said, the benefits of an epidural usually outweigh the potential risks. Talk to your doctor before you make your decision. You'll feel better and more able to make that decision when it comes down to it.

Does an epidural make you too woozy or "out-of-it" to experience the birth fully?

No. The epidural numbs you only from the waist down, and has no effect on your brain. And it doesn't leave you numb for very long after you're finished delivering. The average epidural wears off one to two hours after the anesthesia is stopped.

Is it safe for my baby?

Yes. Unlike some other methods of pain relief such as morphine or Demerol, an epidural does not cross the placenta or affect your baby.

Food might not be your friend (but it is for your partner)

When our mothers gave birth, it was almost universally thought that women in labor should refrain from eating or drinking anything. But today, most doctors are okay with clear liquids and broths—and some will even be okay with a bowl of plain pasta (no meatball subs, though!).

While you may be eating ice chips instead of ice cream, your partner, or whoever your biggest cheerleader is in that delivery room, is going to need all the energy he or she can get right now and should definitely be munching whenever the urge strikes. I'm not saying you should wait in line at the drive-thru to get your partner a burger on the way to the hospital (you're maybe in a little bit of a hurry then!), but remember all those snacks and goodies we packed in your hospital bag? He's going to need them to stay powered up and ready to help you through even the toughest moments—especially if your baby is making his or her arrival in the wee hours of the morning. And don't forget your doctor and the nurses—if your husband goes out to get some food, ask them if they'd like some, too. It can't hurt to have a well-fed team!

C-section survival

I've never actually had a cesarean section (it's one of very few things in pregnancy and motherhood that I haven't been through!), but many of my girlfriends and clients have had them. The main thing I know is that having a C-section instead of vaginal birth doesn't make having your baby any less special—and anyone who says otherwise is clearly certifiable. You can still make the experience personal by bringing your partner, making a special playlist and having it played in the room (Dr. Grunebaum likes to play "Beautiful Day" by U2 when nothing else is requested—so fitting, right?), and taking pictures after the baby is born. You're still going through a lot to have your baby, and in the end, you still get to hold that little babe in your arms and discover so many amazing things about each other—regardless of how he or she came into this world.

So if you need to have a C-section, please, *please* do not be disappointed or feel robbed of something precious. I promise you, the end result is just as sweet, and it's truly only the end result—*your baby!*—that matters in this situation.

That said, if you are choosing to have a C-section without medical indications, I do encourage you to take a step back and think about why you're doing this. C-sections are of course quite safe now, but they are *still* surgical procedures, and deciding to have one for cosmetic or other reasons is highly controversial, when not flat-out frowned upon. I urge you to make the decision based on your baby's needs and what might be best for him or her.

Now, I'll leave you in the hands of a true pro who really knows what happens during a C-section!

PAGING DR. GRUNEBAUM

How does a C-section happen—step-by-step?

C-section delivery is usually done in the operating room. If you were in labor and require a C-section, you will be moved from the labor room to the operating room and put on an operating table. Of course, you may have your partner, or someone else close to you, accompany you to the operating room for support and to observe the birth.

If you already have an epidural with a catheter in place, the anesthesiologist will inject more local anesthesia. If you did not have an epidural, most doctors will administer a spinal anesthesia for the C-section, where the anesthetic is injected directly into the spinal canal. It is very rare for a woman to require a general anesthetic for a C-section, and it will be given only if the surgery has to be done immediately and there is no time to administer an epidural.

Once the anesthetic has been given, your abdomen is cleaned, and an antiseptic solution is applied to the lower abdomen. At this time, a bit of pubic hair will be shaved in the area surrounding where the incision will be made. A catheter will also be placed in the bladder for urine drainage during the surgery.

The doctor will place a screen across your belly so you do not see the surgery as it's happening. The doctor will most typically open the abdomen with a horizontal incision, just above the pubic bone, and then make the incision into the uterus, which is also usually horizontal. After the uterus has been opened, the fetal membranes are incised, and the baby is delivered. If you feel anything during the delivery, it's usually a sensation of slight pressure.

I have heard some crazy rumors that a mother's organs are sometimes "taken out" and then replaced during the process of C-section delivery, but that is absolutely not true! The only things taken out are the baby and the placenta.

Once the baby is out, the umbilical cord will be clamped and cut, and the placenta is delivered. Your partner can snap photos, and you'll be able to see your new son or daughter, too.

At this point, the uterus is closed with a suture, and then the abdomen is closed as well. Your skin is the last step, and can be closed either with staples that will be removed before you are discharged or with stitches that dissolve by themselves.

If you feel pain in your shoulder or arm, it may be because some nerves that travel to that part of your body were affected by the surgery. Tell your doctor, who can give you medication to help you feel more comfortable.

After an uncomplicated C-section, many hospitals will allow mothers to eat and walk around the same day. Mothers are typically kept in the hospital for about four days after the C-section is completed.

Having a baby, step-by-step

Well, beautiful, you're ready for the big time—and it's my job to give you the straight deets, no sugar-coating allowed. Here's how it's all going to go down:

Okay, so that's not really how it goes! I'm going to sign off here for a moment and let Dr. G take over. After all, he's delivered over 3,000 babies—including my own!—so I think he knows this better than anyone.

PAGING DR. GRUNEBAUM

Can you tell me what happens in vaginal delivery—step by step?

There are three stages of labor. In the first stage, your cervix is thinning (effacing) and opening (dilating) because of uterine contractions. This latent phase of the first stage of labor can last anywhere from 12 to 24 hours, but is sometimes shorter if you have previously delivered a baby vaginally. When you have had any signs of labor, which we've gone over previously, you must call your doctor. Depending on your circumstances, your doctor may ask you to come in right away or tell you to spend some of this early stage of labor at home. There are even some cases in which your doctor will have you come in to see if the baby's heart rate is stable, and then send you home for a while. Because every pregnancy

---

is different, I cannot predict what your doctor will want you to do, or generalize about what might be right in your case—but I can say that every woman really must hop on the phone and speak to her doctor to get his or her opinion.

The second, or active, phase of the first stage of labor usually begins when the mother's cervix has dilated to three to four centimeters. At that point, the cervix will usually dilate about one more centimeter each hour. Women who have had previous vaginal deliveries may dilate much faster. The third and final phase of this first stage is the time when labor slows down a little bit, from when you are eight to nine centimeters dilated until you are fully dilated. At this point, the doctor may be checking your dilation about once or twice an hour, depending on your circumstances.

Once your cervix is fully dilated to 10 centimeters, the second stage begins, where the baby will be ready to enter the pelvis and eventually be delivered. It is important, however, to wait for the doctor's advice on when to start pushing. Most doctors believe you should not push right away, but wait until you start to feel more pelvic pressure. The reason is that before entering your pelvis, the baby needs to adjust his or her position to fit through most effectively. If you start pushing too early, you could interfere with this positioning.

Once you are advised to start pushing, there are many ways and different positions in which pushing can happen. You should tell your doctor if you want to move or try a different position. Your doctor is there to help you.

Pushing can be done with every contraction or every other contraction, depending on the circumstances of your individual delivery and your doctor's advice. The whole process may take several hours.

As the baby gets closer to being born, many women (even those with an epidural) may feel more pressure on the perineum. Sometimes your doctor will tell you to stop pushing in order to prevent the perineum being torn.

Today, routine episiotomies are a thing of the past, but they are still done in cases where the woman is exhausted and a quicker delivery is advised, or in cases where the baby's heart rate is abnormal.

Once the baby's head emerges from the vagina, the doctor will feel to see if the umbilical cord is wrapped around the baby's neck, which happens in roughly one-third of births. If that is the case, the doctor may slide the cord over the baby's head or clamp and cut the cord early on. Again, at this point, the doctor may advise you to stop pushing.

Once the baby's head emerges, the rest of the baby will usually be born within 30 to 60 seconds. You can request to have your baby placed on your stomach while the doctor clamps and cuts the umbilical cord. It is essential that the baby is dried and covered as soon as he or she is born, because the temperature in the room is much colder than the temperatures in the womb.

Roughly 30 to 60 seconds after the baby is born, the baby will take his or her first breath. In one minute after birth, and again five minutes after birth, the baby will receive an Apgar score of zero, one, or two in five different parameters, with a total maximum score of 10. This score is given to confirm whether the baby requires extra breathing support in the hospital. There is no correlation between a high Apgar score and whether or not your child will get into Harvard or Yale!

Meanwhile, you have entered the third and final stage of labor, where the placenta is delivered. Waiting for the placenta to emerge can take up to 30 minutes. When the placenta has separated from the uterus and is being delivered, you will feel pressure, and some women say it feels almost like another baby is going to be born, but the placenta is usually delivered much quicker than a baby!

After the placenta is delivered, Pitocin is often given to help the uterus contract, and to prevent excessive bleeding. The doctor will also examine you for any tears and repair those and any episiotomy that may have been done with stitches if necessary. If you had an epidural, you can have more anesthetic for this; and if you have not had an epidural, you can still request local anesthetic at this point to help you through the stitching.

Most new mothers go home one to two days after giving birth vaginally.

10 gross things nobody will notice (and you probably don't want to share)

Okay, the truth is that I tried to think of 10 gross things, and really? There's only one.

Le deux.

Or, if we're being a bit less delicate, poo. The stories you've heard are flat-out true—you will almost definitely go number two while pushing through labor. In fact, it means you're pushing well, as pushing should feel like you're . . . working really hard at doing your *business*.

But the thing is, you won't necessarily feel it come out in the first place—and nobody is going to be rude enough to say anything (could you imagine!). All of the doctors and nurses and midwives and doulas in the world have seen this happen so many times that it doesn't even faze them—and if you're giving birth in the hospital or at a birthing center, some nice person will swiftly fly to your side, clean it up, and get it taken immediately away, like it never happened. Magic!

Besides, when the beautiful, healthy baby emerges from you, everyone will be so moved and overwhelmed with excitement that any memory of what came out of you *before* will be gone in a flash. I'll pinky swear to that one.

PAGING DR. GRUNEBAUM

Is there any way to prevent pooing in
the delivery room?

Yes, there can be a way to avoid a bowel movement during delivery—
although it really is no big deal. Doctors see these every day; they are natural

---

and nothing to be ashamed of. Still, some doctors will advise that women who are worried about having a bowel movement give themselves an enema at home to clear their bowels before coming to the hospital—but this is not for everyone to do. You really should talk to your doctor and discuss whether or not he or she advises an enema in your situation.

Baby mine (or, um, yours!)

You've been through so much together already. You've protected, championed, fed, and talked to this mysterious little babe since before he or she even had fingernails, and he or she has been kicking and twisting and stretching inside you—perhaps mainly to get your attention! Finally now, today, you can look each other in the eye and feel the overwhelming and unique bond that exists only between a mother and her child.

Some mothers like to have their baby whisked away to the nursery for a bit right after giving birth so they can rest—and if you're one of them, more power to you, but I've never been able to part with my babies that quickly. I hold them on my chest and can't stop marveling at that magically soft skin, those impossibly small toes.

Take time to really enjoy this moment. You've earned it, and it is one of the most incredible rushes you will ever feel in your lifetime.

Who's in your tribe?

You've already got:

- ○ Your partner and/or your or best friend
- ○ Your doctor or midwife
- ○ Your parents and in-laws
- ○ A mommy workout buddy
- ○ An all-star event planner
- ○ Your birth and parenting teachers
- ○ You (you're the most important member, silly!)
- ○ Your group of close friends
- ○ Your lactation consultant if you're breastfeeding
- ○ The delivery guy at your favorite takeout spot (you'll get to know him well!)

And you're adding:

- ○ The hospital or birthing center staff (unless you're having a home birth)
- ○ Your baby!

Murmurs from the Man Cave

You've made it all the way through, hand in hand, and together you're about to be *parents*. Yes, you're the one who has actually given birth to that little dream inside you, but don't think the wonder of it all is lost on your partner. Here are some things the guys in our Man Cave had to say about the most important day of all.

"It was and still is the most amazing moment of my life. Words cannot describe how magical it was."

"The moment I held my son, my whole life suddenly made sense and felt like it had a purpose. I didn't expect that and wasn't emotionally prepared to feel that rush."

"I'm not normally an emotional guy, but I was so over-whelmed by emotion. It was the coolest moment in my life. When they gave me my baby and I had him in my arms for the first time, I'd never felt more love or more proud about anything in my life."

The takeaway

Babies are magical. They bring out the best in all of us, and help us see our true potential. Being a parent isn't always easy, but it truly is one of the greatest privileges life has to offer. Enjoy it, and share this wonderful moment together as one big, *beautiful* family.

Count to 14 and Everything Will Be Okay:

getting through the first two weeks

Dear Lovely,

You've done it—you've given birth to a squirmy, stretchy, fussy, absolutely gorgeous little miracle! You're a mommy—and for that, you should feel fantastic. I'm immensely proud of you and hope you are proud of yourself. Perhaps someday soon (if it hasn't happened already!) I'll get to meet you and that sweet little bundle, too.

So now that the "hard part" is over, why isn't everything perfect, you ask? Why aren't all the cute forest animals from Bambi circling around to welcome your new babe (soundly asleep in the bassinet, of course) as your flowing hair blows in the breeze and you stand there proudly in your skinniest skinny jeans? Because these first 14 days just aren't that easy for any of us.

No matter how in love you are with that precious little pumpkin of yours, the first two weeks especially can be just plain difficult. Maybe you're overwhelmed with all the new responsibilities (I can remember breaking down over whether or not I was feeding my babies enough and about a billion other things!), still feeling a bit split in two from giving birth, or maybe you're just plain out-and-out tired (likely a combination of all three!). All of these feelings are 100 percent okay—normal, and even expected.

Nobody talks about this because it's not the picture-perfect image of new motherhood we've been told about, but you're not alone. And I swear that it will get better every day—and while it's not always easy, parenting is truly the greatest privilege in life. You *will* figure it out. Maybe not by day one, day five, or even by day 12. But by day 14, the light will start to shine through again and you'll start to feel like *you* again (Remember you? That fabulous, clever, passionate woman you used to see in the mirror? You haven't lost a bit of her—she just needs a few days to recoup, and in time, you'll become an even better version of her!). Things really will start to feel possible again.

You should plan on doing nothing these first two weeks but taking care of yourself and your new little love—advice that I've learned not only through my own experiences, but though those of so many of my amazing clients. Work can wait. If you don't feel like having visitors, they can wait, too (to heck with their protestations—you just gave birth, you call the shots!). And as for any big decisions or changes? Absolutely put them off until at least day 14. This isn't the time for any of that.

The most you can really ask of yourself is to get up every day, make sure your little one is safe, fed, and clean, and try to at least put a comb through your own hair—let's be honest, you won't be washing it as much as you'd like, if at all! It's really just one foot in front of the other at this point, and who cares if you don't get dressed until four in the afternoon . . . three days from now.

That said, if anything seems unbearable, or you're having emotions or urges that scare you, call your doctor and tell him or her what's going on. There's no shame in asking for help or in not waiting for your six-week checkup—in fact, it just shows that you're already an amazing parent, and using all the resources you've got to ensure your little one has a healthy start.

So, mark off those calendar days and count to 14. When these two weeks are over, everything will seem a bit more under control. Queen Victoria will be on the road to mending (unimaginable, but it actually will happen), you'll be a little more used to the sleepless nights, you'll be a diaper-changing wiz, your bodacious boobs will either be getting into a breastfeeding rhythm or starting to understand you aren't actually going to be breastfeeding, you might have had a shower or two—and even discovered that you can see your toes again as your belly goes down.

Hang in there. This first bit can be a bit bumpy, I know, but your life from here on out is going to be so full of wonder and magic that it's all worth it—because you, my friend, are a *mother* and you are holding your baby right there in your arms.

Rosie x

HEALTHY EATING FOR TWO WITH ANDREA ORBECK

'm going to hand you off to Andrea again for some fantastically solid advice on what to feed yourself and your growing baby during your pregnancy—she knows what she's talking about! As a friend and colleague of hers, I respect so much Andrea's wisdom and the love she has for mothers and babies. Having said that, I also know that it's not always possible to stick to her absolutely perfect plan (I try to be good, and am good most of the time, but sometimes I swear those cookies just fly into my mouth!). I guess what I'm trying to say is that I'm human and so are you. Don't beat yourself up, but do the best you can. Andrea's recommendations are a phenomenal place to start.

Hello again! Eating healthy is obviously always important, but during pregnancy, it's not just you who will suffer the consequences of skipping breakfast or having a vending-machine lunch—there's a little baby in there who needs (and deserves!) better. After all, your baby's development is directly affected by the nutrients you provide for his or her growth. Think of it this way: everything you eat helps to grow those tiny bones and muscles, and helps to develop that brilliant brain. I'm pretty sure you don't want your baby to be made out of candy bars and nachos—so stick with me and we'll get you all sorted out.

Knowing what to eat when you're pregnant can seem complicated, but it's really not when you remember these simple rules:

1. Try to eat as much natural, non-packaged, non-processed food as possible,

2. get lots of fruits, veggies, and whole grains,

3. and try to limit your sweets and fried food.

I also make the case for eating organic whenever possible. I know it's more expensive, but there are enough studies out there to defend it during pregnancy. What we consume passes through the placenta and is given to our developing and growing babies. If we can avoid unnecessary pesticides, hormones, and genetically modified foods, all the better! Yes, it's an investment, but since you're already refraining from alcohol and severely limiting or omitting coffee altogether, you'll have a little room for your organic baby budget.

There are, of course, some must-have nutrients, but instead of just telling you that you need them, I'm going to tell you why—that always helps me remember things a bit better!

nutrient	why you need it
folic acid/ folate	This helps prevent major birth defects including neural-tube defects, and also helps prevent lower birth weights. You should get a lot of folic acid from food, but you'll also definitely need a supplement.
iron	Iron is what carries oxygen throughout your body. Without enough, we feel woozy and light-headed, and can become anemic. During pregnancy, your iron needs double, since your baby takes whatever he or she needs from what you eat first. Some women need a supplement.
calcium	Calcium needs also double, since all those adorable baby bones are being built out of it! Be careful with calcium, though—don't have it at the same meal as a big iron-booster, as it can prevent your body from absorbing the iron properly.
vitamin d	This vitamin helps your body absorb all that calcium you need for your baby's growth.
vitamin b6	It will boost your energy levels (which can drag during pregnancy!) And has also been shown to help with morning sickness.

nutrient	why you need it
vitamin a	You need this to help the baby's heart, lungs, kidneys, eyes, bones, circulatory system, respiratory system, and nervous system develop properly. Pretty important! Also, it can help you repair any torn or damaged tissues postpartum.
vitamin c	Besides helping with your baby's bone growth and immune system, it also helps your body absorb that iron you're getting. Try to pair vitamin c–rich foods with iron-rich foods for an extra boost.
fiber	All that iron you're having right about now can leave you constipated and uncomfortable without a hefty dose of fiber. Trust me on this one—anything that keeps you "going" is a good thing.
protein	Protein provides the foundation for your baby's growth. Make sure you get plenty!
thiamin	This helps your baby's brain development (hello, smarty!) And also keeps your heart, muscles, and nervous system strong.

nutrient	why you need it
riboflavin	This helps your baby build strong bones, a healthy nervous system, and all those tiny muscles.
phosphorus	Who knew so much went into building bones? This is another major building block for the baby's skeletal system.
potassium	Not only does potassium help your body get the most out of the protein, fats, and carbs you eat, but it also helps prevent painful leg cramps. Ah, sweet relief!
magnesium	This mineral is essential for fetal growth and can help prevent premature labor.
selenium	This helps boost your immune system. Cold and flu, be gone!
omega-3	This one is a biggie for helping your baby's brain be as brilliant as it can be.
omega-6	This one helps you balance your hormones a bit. Got mood swings? Get some omega-6!

Now that you know why you need what you need, here's a quick and easy guide to getting it all in (even on the busiest days!). Need a breakfast idea? Not sure what to nosh for lunch? Scan these lists and you'll be set.

Ready? Set? Yum!

Breakfast—rise and shine, gorgeous!

Breakfast really is the most important meal of the day. You have been sleeping for the last eight hours (we hope!) and during that time, growing a baby! Start the day with tissue-building protein, complex carbs for energy, and fiber and fruit for vitamins and digestion.

Pick and choose from:

Organic nonfat or 1% milk (protein, vitamins)

Almond milk (vitamins D and E, calcium)

Soy milk if you love it, but only organic and nonfat (riboflavin, calcium, protein)

Low-fat organic cottage cheese (protein)

100% whole-wheat bread (fiber, vitamins, minerals)

Sprouted grain breads and tortilla bread—great for breakfast burritos! (fiber, vitamins, minerals)

Whole-grain cereals (fiber, vitamins, minerals)

Bran cereals (fiber, vitamins, minerals)

Oatmeal—plain if instant; you can always add stevia sweetener or fruit and yogurt (fiber, vitamins, minerals)

Cream-of-wheat cereal (vitamin A, calcium, iron)

Yogurt—nonfat, no sugar, but you can add fruit for sweetness and extra
vitamins (protein, calcium, phosphorous)
Egg whites (protein, selenium)
Organic eggs—one yolk per day, max (protein, folic acid, selenium)

To sauté in omelets:

Frozen or fresh spinach (vitamin A, magnesium)
Green, red, and yellow bell peppers (vitamin C)
Onions (fiber, vitamins C and B6, folic acid, potassium)
Low-sodium, organic turkey bacon (phosphorus)

Frozen or fresh organic fruit on its own, mixed in a smoothie, or with yogurt:

Strawberries (vitamin C, fiber)
Blueberries (vitamin C, fiber)
Banana (potassium, vitamin B6, fiber)

Lunch—let's do it!

If you work during the day, start packing a lunch following some of these delicious
ideas. You'll save money, get all the nutrients you and your baby need, and help protect
yourself from the very dangerous and even deadly bacteria that can be found at even
the most established fast-food joints and delis.

For salads:

Organic spring mix with arugula, spinach, and lettuce (vitamin A, folate, fiber)
Celery (fiber, water)
Organic tomatoes (vitamins A and C)
Avocado (vitamins C, E, B6, omega-3, folate, fiber)
Ready-to-eat coleslaw (fiber)
Dried cranberries (vitamin C, magnesium, fiber)
Mixed nuts (protein, folate, thiamin, calcium, magnesium, omega-6)
Pineapple chunks (vitamin C, thiamin, potassium, magnesium)
Raisins (fiber, omega-6)
Organic chicken breast (protein, niacin, vitamin B6, selenium)
Organic turkey breast (protein, niacin, vitamin B6, selenium)

For sandwiches:

100% whole-wheat bread (fiber, vitamins, minerals)
100% whole-wheat buns or pita (selenium, magnesium, fiber, vitamins)
Low-fat, non-processed, pasteurized cheeses—skim mozzarella is good,
    shredded or sliced (protein, calcium)
Organic chicken breast (protein, niacin, vitamin B6, selenium)
Organic turkey breast (protein, niacin, vitamin B6, selenium)
Organic tomatoes (vitamins A and C)
Avocado (vitamins C, E, and B6, omega-3, folate, fiber)

Hearty, organic, low-sodium soups:

Tomato (vitamins A and C)
Vegetable (vitamin A and fiber)
Bean (fiber, iron, folate, protein, magnesium)
Chili (fiber, iron, folate, protein, magnesium)

Fruit for dessert—fresh or frozen, never canned or in syrup!
(vitamins A, C, fiber, and more):

Peaches	Cherries	Apples
Pears	Strawberries	Oranges
Grapes	Pineapple	Nectarines
Blueberries	Bananas	Apricots

Dinner—time to wind down!

Dinner is a great time to get tons of nutrients in, but if you're having trouble sleeping or have been experiencing heartburn, try to eat at least a few hours before bed. If your body's still digesting when you lie down, it can lead to troublesome rest.

Pick and choose from:

Organic breast of chicken or turkey (protein, niacin, vitamin B6, selenium)
Fish—6 ounces, twice a week from these low-mercury sources:

> *butterfish, catfish, clams, crab, flounder, haddock, salmon, scallops, squid, tilapia, trout (protein, omega-3, omega-6, vitamins, minerals—especially B vitamins, selenium, and pantothenic acid)

Lean beef (protein, iron, zinc, selenium, niacin, vitamin B6)
Lean pork (protein, thiamin, niacin, vitamin B6)
Lean lamb (protein, zinc, niacin, vitamin B6)

Brown rice—keeps you full much longer than white rice! (iron, vitamin B6, magnesium, fiber)

Quinoa—a versatile and tasty grain (protein, good carbs, folate, B vitamins)

100% whole-wheat pasta (fiber, vitamins, minerals)

Aramanth (calcium, fiber, iron)

Barley (fiber, niacin, iron)

Bulgur (fiber, folate)

Mixed green salad (vitamin A, folate, fiber)

Green and yellow beans (fiber)

Peas (fiber)

Lentils (protein, thiamin, folate, niacin, vitamin B6, fiber, iron, magnesium, potassium)

Squash (fiber, vitamin C)

Spinach (vitamin A, iron)

Broccoli (vitamins A and C, folate, iron)

Kale (lots of iron, vitamin A)

Asparagus (fiber, iron)

Avocado (vitamins C, E, and B6, omega-3, folate, fiber)

Organic soybeans—these pack twice as much protein as red meat or cheese! (protein, calcium, phosphorus, vitamin B)

Chard (vitamins A and C, calcium, iron)

Bean soups and chilis (fiber, iron, folate, protein, magnesium)

Snacks—who can live without 'em?

Snacks are important because they can help curb voracious cravings or help settle the stomach when needed. Having little protein snacks is healthy if your stomach can handle it, and frequent dry nibbles like crackers can always help if you need something to absorb troublesome acid in your tummy.

Pick and choose from:

Walnuts (high in omega-3, protein)
Almonds (vitamin E, riboflavin, folate, magnesium)
Almond butter (vitamin E, riboflavin, folate, magnesium)
Celery (fiber, water)
Whole-wheat crackers (fiber, vitamins, minerals)
All fruit (fiber, vitamins A and C, and so much more!)
Chopped vegetable platter (fiber, vitamins A and C, and so much more!)

ROSIE'S NO-FRILLS GEAR GUIDE

New moms are so excited to do everything right (and rightfully so!), which is why so many stores will try to sell you absolutely everything they can right now—including some pretty nutso stuff that *nobody* needs. That's why I thought I'd make it simple for you. Here are the absolute basics you'll need to get started, with just a few "nice to haves" thrown in. And if heading to the store seems a bit overwhelming? Put on some music, put your feet up, and head online. It's just as easy as that!

From day one you'll need . . .

Layette

- ◯ Swaddle cloths
- ◯ Onesies (10)
- ◯ Body suits (10)
- ◯ Socks (7)
- ◯ Hats (2–3)
- ◯ Gowns (5)
- ◯ Kimono pant sets (5)
- ◯ Mittens (1 pair)
- ◯ Bibs (8–12)
- ◯ Burping cloths (6–12)

Sleeping

- ◯ Crib with a mattress
- ◯ Bassinet
- ◯ Crib sheets—four sets

Feeding

- ◯ Breast pads
- ◯ Breast cream
- ◯ Breast milk storage containers or bags
- ◯ Nursing bra
- ◯ 4- or 5-oz bottles (6–8)
- ◯ Slow-flow nipples
- ◯ Bottle sterilizer
- ◯ Bottle brush
- ◯ Hypoallergenic bottle wash
- ◯ Sterilizing microwave steam bags
- ◯ Formula if not breastfeeding

Diapering

- ◯ Diapers
- ◯ Baby wipes
- ◯ Diaper bag with changing pad
- ◯ Diaper rash cream
- ◯ Diaper pail
- ◯ Diaper pail refills

Bathing

- ○ Baby bath tub
- ○ Washcloths (6)
- ○ Baby body wash
- ○ Baby shampoo
- ○ Baby lotion

Health and Hygiene

- ○ Hypoallergenic detergent
- ○ Hand sanitizer
- ○ Nail clippers
- ○ Brush and comb
- ○ Digital thermometer
- ○ First aid kit
- ○ Aquaphor

Safety

- ○ Interference-free monitor
- ○ Smoke and carbon monoxide alarm

Travel and Play

- ○ Infant car seat (snap-and-go or adaptable stroller)
- ○ Stroller (the type depends on your lifestyle)
- ○ Stroller rain cover
- ○ Stroller sleeping bag
- ○ Jungle gym

You might want, but don't *have* to have . . .

For the Nursery

○ Changing table/dresser with a pad and four covers

○ Glider

Feeding

○ Breast pump

○ Bottle drying rack

○ Breastfeeding shawl

○ Pacifiers (6–8)

○ Nursing pillow

Travel and Play

○ Front and hip carriers

○ Stroller toys

○ Wrap carriers

○ Full-size swing

○ Stroller organizer

○ Travel swing

○ Stroller cup holder

○ Crib mobile

You'll need these things later . . .

Feeding

○ 8-, 9-, or 11-oz. bottles (6–8)

○ High chair

○ Medium flow nipples

○ Teethers

○ Fast flow nipples

Safety

- ○ Cabinet and door safety latches
- ○ Safety gates
- ○ Outlet covers
- ○ Edge guards

Travel and Play

- ○ Activity jumper
- ○ Mobile walker
- ○ Crib toys
- ○ Activity and story books
- ○ Toy box
- ○ Play mat
- ○ Bath toys
- ○ DVDs and CDs
- ○ Rattles

TRICKY BITS WITH
DR. GRUNEBAUM

Sometimes things come up in pregnancy that are immensely difficult, both emotionally and physically. Because they are of paramount importance to the women who go through them, I wanted to dedicate a space in the book entirely to these challenges.

I sincerely wish that there was a way I could ensure every pregnancy went smoothly and resulted in a healthy birth—but because my own experiences have been troubled, I know firsthand how helpless and lost you can feel when things aren't going right. I also know that when I've felt scared, or have just received devastating news, knowing the facts has given me a bit of clarity and helped make things feel at least a little less out of control.

For that reason, I've asked Dr. Grunebaum, who specializes in high-risk pregnancy and deals with these challenging moments on a daily basis, to take over here and tell you everything you need to know about some of the hardest moments in pregnancy. By no means is this a complete list of the complications and challenges that may arise, but I hope it's helpful to those who need it.

Miscarriage

How common are miscarriages?

Most women don't realize that a very high percentage of pregnancies—30 to 40 percent, to be exact—do not survive to full term. Most of these miscarriages happen before week 12, and they are more likely in women over age 35.

How can I prevent a miscarriage?

Most miscarriages are due to chromosomal flukes in the pregnancy that cannot be prevented, but there are ways to decrease the risk overall. Taking prenatal vitamins from before the time you even become pregnant or as soon as possible is important, as folic acid can decrease your risk. Also, of course, a no-smoking, no-drinking, no- or low-caffeine diet, and being watchful of eating recommended foods in pregnancy will help.

Are there any symptoms I should watch for?

Many miscarriages start with vaginal bleeding or spotting, while others are not associated with any specific symptoms and are found only when the doctor does a sonogram and does not see a fetal heartbeat.

What is done when a pregnancy miscarries?

Treatment can include either waiting for the pregnancy to pass spontaneously, administering medication that will help your body push out the pregnancy, or performing a D and C, or uterine scraping, to remove the fetal tissue from your body.

If I've had a miscarriage, will I ever be successfully pregnant again?

Having a miscarriage does not affect your future fertility. If you've had one, your chances of miscarrying again are no higher than anyone else's.

Ectopic pregnancy

What is it?

Ectopic pregnancy is a pregnancy that implants outside the mother's uterus—where a fetus cannot thrive or grow properly. These pregnancies cannot survive to term, and the cells that are developing must be removed to save the woman's life. Ectopic pregnancies can occur in the cervix, in the fallopian tubes, or occasionally in an ovary or in the abdominal cavity.

How common is it?

Somewhere between one in 60 and one in 80 pregnancies are ectopic, but the risk is increased in women with a history of pelvic infections and especially in women who have previously experienced an ectopic pregnancy. Women who have had surgery on their fallopian tubes or ovaries are also at a higher risk.

What signs should I look for?

If you have previously had an ectopic pregnancy and have a positive pregnancy test, you should be seen by your doctor immediately and have an early ultrasound to rule out another ectopic pregnancy. Similarly, if you have missed your period and have a positive pregnancy test but are experiencing pain in your lower abdomen and some vaginal spotting, you also need to be seen right away so the doctor can confirm whether the pregnancy is located inside your uterus or outside. This can be done either through an ultrasound or a blood test.

What needs to be done?

If an ectopic pregnancy is diagnosed early on, and it has not ruptured, it can be treated with minimally invasive surgery, without a large incision. There is also a kind of chemotherapy that can be injected to help remove the ectopic pregnancy. If the ectopic pregnancy ruptures, the woman carrying it can go into shock and would need emergency surgery to remove the pregnancy.

What does it mean for my fertility?

Having an ectopic pregnancy does not mean you'll never give birth to a healthy baby. Rosie is proof of this! That said, it does make it harder to get pregnant in the future and raises your risk of having another ectopic pregnancy. For many women, IVF is a good way to get pregnant after an ectopic pregnancy, as the process bypasses the fallopian tubes entirely, which reduces your risk. Still, IVF is not always necessary to ensure future pregnancies.

Genetic abnormalities

What genetic abnormalities are being tested for?

The nuchal scan or early fetal screening, along with the CVS (chorionic villus sampling) and amniocentesis tests, help determine the likelihood that the fetus growing inside you is affected by genetic issues such as Down syndrome, Turner syndrome, Edward syndrome, and congenital heart defects.

What if I would rather not know?

No one can force you into having these tests done, nor should anyone—this is a very personal decision. However, if you or your doctor feel you are at higher risk for genetic abnormalities, it can be helpful to know the likelihood of an issue so you can learn and prepare your family for the challenges that will occur later on. If your child will have difficulties immediately after birth, it can be vital to have pediatric surgeons and other specialists on board and ready to help.

What do the numbers mean?

There is risk for genetic abnormality in all pregnancies, but if a test comes back with less than a one-in-350 likelihood, many doctors will say your baby is more than likely healthy and without abnormality. That said, a ratio that indicates a higher likelihood does not mean that there is an issue, either. You really must speak to your doctor and genetic counselor about the results and decide what the numbers mean to you in your life and in your situation.

What are the options if my child is at high risk for abnormalities?

You have three options to discuss with your doctor. Those are to continue the pregnancy without question, to watch the pregnancy closely for issues and decide what to do as those arise, or to terminate the pregnancy. Again, these are intensely personal decisions that should be made in concert with your partner or close support system, with input from your medical team.

Multiples

If I want to have twins, what are some tips that might increase my chances?

Many women think having twins or triplets is a wonderful way to create their whole family in one pregnancy. However, there are very serious complications and risks involved with having multiples. When a mother carries more than one fetus, it is less likely that she will be able to carry that pregnancy to term, and if she does, those children may be sick. These are important things to know and consider.

What are the risks involved with carrying multiples?

Most twins and multiples are delivered earlier than single babies. They are usually healthy, but in general, they have a higher risk of having cerebral palsy and other complications. The mothers are at higher risk for gestational diabetes, and are more likely to need a C-section delivery.

I plan to do IVF, which often results in multiples. What should I know?

Talk to your IVF doctor and ask if he or she thinks it's advisable to implant just *one* embryo—rather than two or more. If more than one embryo is implanted, there is an increased chance of twins. Most women seeking IVF aren't aware of the increased risk, and for them it's more important to get pregnant in the first place than it is to prevent multiples. That said, IVF techniques are so good today that having multiple embryos implanted instead of one does not necessarily increase your chances of pregnancy—it simply increases your chance of becoming pregnant with multiples. It is crucial to speak up before the procedure and specify that you want only one embryo implanted. In fact, implanting more than one embryo at a time through IVF is illegal in some European countries because of the risks it poses to the mother's health and the implications for the pregnancy overall.

I'm pregnant with multiples. What can I do to help my chances of a healthy birth?

Twins occur naturally in one out of every 80 pregnancies, and it is important to note that those pregnancies often require closer monitoring and increased contact with the medical team. The first thing to ask your doctor is whether or not the fetuses share a placenta; the medical term for this is monochorionic. If the answer is yes, you may need to seek the help of a maternal-fetal medical specialist, or MFM. MFMs (like myself!) are very experienced in monitoring high-risk births and will know what to do at every step to increase your chances of delivering healthy babies. Healthy multiples are born every day, but you will have a more difficult pregnancy than most.

Even if the fetuses do not share a placenta, you will need to be monitored much more closely than a woman pregnant with only one child to address any risks of premature labor. Your cervix will be measured frequently, and you may have ultrasounds every two to four weeks to check the health of your pregnancy. Pregnancies in which multiples are involved are always more complicated and difficult to endure, so make sure you have a medical team you trust and with whom you feel comfortable.

Rh negative disease

What is it, and how do I know if my baby is at risk?

There are four blood types people can have: O, A, B, or AB; each person also is either "positive" or "negative" in reference to the Rh (rhesus) proteins on the surface of the blood cells. The majority of people are Rh positive—your doctor will know whether you are Rh positive or negative from routine blood testing.

If an Rh negative woman has a baby with an Rh positive man, the baby has a good chance of being Rh positive. Women who are Rh negative, regardless of whether they are O, A, B, or AB, can create antibodies during pregnancy that can cross the placenta and attack the baby's red blood cells if the baby she is carrying is Rh positive. This can make the baby anemic, and in severe cases, the baby will go into heart failure.

What can be done?

All women who are Rh negative are tested during pregnancy to see if they are at risk of attacking the baby's red blood cells. If they are, they are given an injection of a medication called RhoGAM, which masks the baby's red blood cells so the mother's body does not detect them.

Will my Rh status affect my baby's health?

If you are monitored and given proper treatment for Rh negative disease, then your baby will not be affected.

Group B strep

What is Group B strep, how common is it, and how will I know if I have it?

Group B strep (GBS) is a bacterium that can be found in the rectum or vagina of one in every four women. Most women with GBS do not have any symptoms, and often have no idea that they are carrying it, which is why all women are tested with a vaginal and rectal swab between 35 and 37 weeks of their pregnancy.

What does it mean for my baby, and what can be done?

If a woman carries GBS, there is a very small chance (roughly five out of 10,000 deliveries) that it may be transferred to her baby. To prevent that, mothers with GBS are given an antibiotic intravenously when they go into labor.

Uterine infections

What is a uterine infection, and why does it happen?

Uterine infections, also called chorioamnionitis, are infections of the placenta or membranes surrounding the baby. These are more likely to happen when the amniotic sac is prematurely ruptured and bacteria get into the uterus.

What are the risks involved with uterine infections?

Uterine infections are a major cause of premature labor and often lead to babies being born early. If these infections are allowed to progress, the mother can develop an infection in her blood called sepsis, which can severely harm her organs, and in the most extreme cases, lead to her death.

What are signs that I might have a uterine infection?

Uterine infections are most highly associated with an early rupture of membranes, so regardless of when it happens, make sure to call your doctor when your water breaks. Other signs include a fever, foul-smelling discharge, or uterine tenderness in the mother, and occasionally an increased heart rate in the baby.

What can be done?

Women with uterine infections are usually delivered quickly, regardless of how far along they are in their pregnancy. This is to reduce the risk of death in the mother. Once the baby is delivered, and the fetal membranes and placenta have left the mother's body, the infection is usually gone within 24 to 48 hours.

Preeclampsia

What exactly is preeclampsia?

Preeclampsia is a condition unique to pregnancy associated with high blood pressure and protein in a mother's urine. It increases health risks to both the baby and the mother to the point where the mother could die if it is not treated. If left alone, preeclampsia can elevate to eclampsia, wherein mothers experience seizures and sometimes strokes.

What are the signs or symptoms to watch for?

High or elevated blood pressure is the number-one sign, which is why your doctor will check your blood pressure every time you come in for an appointment. The other way doctors look for this is by screening your urine sample to see if it contains protein. Additional signs include sudden weight gain, severe headaches, abdominal pain, and any other sudden and drastic changes during pregnancy.

Are some women more at risk than others?

Preeclampsia can occur in any pregnancy, but some women are at a higher risk. These include women with their first pregnancy, women who are obese, women who are carrying multiples, women with diabetes or hypertension, and those who have had preeclampsia in previous pregnancies. If your doctor diagnoses you with preeclampsia, it can worsen and turn into eclampsia, preeclampsia along with seizures. Eclampsia has much higher risks to the life of the mother.

What does it mean for my baby's health?

When a mother has preeclampsia, her baby may not grow at a normal rate, and may not be getting enough nutrients from the mother. In extreme cases, this can lead to stillbirth.

What can be done?

The only treatment for preeclampsia is delivery, which if it happens prematurely can increase the child's risk of respiratory difficulties and other health issues—but may save the mother's life. If the preeclampsia occurs early on in the pregnancy and is mild, the doctor may sometimes recommend very close observation, either on bed rest or in the hospital, until the baby is more mature and equipped for life outside the womb.

Placenta previa

What is placenta previa, how common is it, and who is most at risk?

Early in pregnancy, it's normal for the placenta to be close to the cervix, but as the baby grows and the uterus stretches, the placenta normally grows up and away from the cervix. Placenta previa is a complication wherein the placenta remains implanted in the low part of the uterus later in pregnancy and covers part or all of the cervix—partially or fully blocking the baby's way out.

Placenta previa happens in roughly one out of every 200 pregnancies, and is more common in women who have had surgery on the uterus, women who smoke, older mothers, and those who have had placenta previa in previous pregnancies.

What can be done?

There is nothing that can be done to prevent placenta previa, but once a woman is diagnosed with it, she will be told not to have sexual intercourse. This is because when the penis moves in the direction of the cervix, it can detatch the placenta, which can lead to premature birth. Most women with placenta previa have a C-section performed before 38 weeks of pregnancy.

Do I need to see a specialist?

Discuss this with your doctor. Some doctors are more experienced with placenta previa than others and feel confident overseeing pregnancies affected by it. Others may wish you to see a specialist who has more knowledge and expertise in this area.

Preterm labor and birth

What is considered premature birth, and why is it such a big deal?

Premature birth or preterm birth is when the baby is born before 37 weeks, or more than three weeks before the due date—and it is the number-one event that harms babies. Babies that are born prematurely may need assistance breathing or experience bleeding in the brain, among other complications; some do not survive.

Who is at risk for premature birth?

Premature birth could happen in virtually any pregnancy, but women who are at highest risk include those with a history of premature birth, women who are pregnant with multiples, and women who have diabetes or hypertension.

What are some signs or symptoms of premature labor?

Some signs that you may be in premature labor include experiencing any of the following before 37 weeks:

- a change in vaginal discharge
- pelvic or abdominal pressure
- vaginal bleeding
- a low-back ache
- menstrual-like cramping or rhythmic cramps like contractions

If you feel any of these before 37 weeks, call your doctor immediately, as you may be going into premature labor and need immediate care. If you wait too long to call or go to the hospital, you may not be able to receive appropriate treatment.

If you do get to the hospital early on in preterm labor, your doctor may be able to medically stop the labor, preventing a premature birth. There is also a medication your doctor can administer directly to the baby, which can prevent some of the negative physical effects of premature labor in the event of a preterm birth. This must be given a few hours before delivery, so it's of the utmost importance to notify your doctor immediately of anything that might be a symptom of premature labor.

I've gone into premature labor before—will it happen again?

If you've had a history of premature labor, you may want to seek the help of a maternal fetal medicine specialist who is well versed in high-risk births, although it is not always necessary to do so. There are different things your doctor can do in the next pregnancy to decrease your risk. New research urges doctors treating women at high risk for premature birth to measure the length of their cervix at around 20 weeks to determine the risks of another premature delivery. If the doctor deems that risk high, vaginal suppositories, which can decrease the risk of having another premature baby, can be given once a week. These are safe and will not affect your baby—in fact, they will help your baby tremendously if they prevent a premature birth.

V-BAC: vaginal birth after cesarean section

If I've had a C-section, can I deliver my next child vaginally?

When a woman has had a C-section, there is a chance that her uterus will rupture in future pregnancies, which makes another C-section necessary. That said, if the incision from your C-section was performed horizontally in the lower part of the uterus (as most incisions are!), your risk of uterine rupture in future pregnancies is less than 2 percent. If your incision is in the upper section of your uterus, your risk of uterine rupture is much higher, and most doctors will not recommend future vaginal deliveries.

If you gave birth vaginally in a pregnancy prior to or subsequent to your C-section, your chances of successfully delivering vaginally once again are very high. If you have never delivered vaginally, your chances are still good, at about a 60 to 70 percent success rate.

You should discuss your wishes to have a V-BAC with your doctor early on in your pregnancy, so he or she can assess the risks and talk them over with you.

Do I need to see a specialist?

You do not need to see a specialist, but you will need to come to the hospital earlier on in your labor than most women.

In what case would I need to have another C-section?

If the uterine incision from your previous C-section is vertical or in the upper part of your uterus, most doctors will insist upon performing a C-section for your next birth.

In mothers where a V-BAC is attempted, the baby's heart rate will be monitored very closely, as an abnormal heart rate is the first sign of uterine rupture. In cases of uterine rupture, emergency C-sections are performed immediately to preserve the health of the mother and baby.

ACKNOWLEDGMENTS

When writing a book such as this about pregnancy, one of the most blessed and life-changing things a woman can go through, it is hard to know where to begin with the thanks. I suppose that I would like to thank in some way everybody that I have come into contact with on this journey into motherhood, and into my career, for teaching me something, provoking a thought, or motivating me to do it my way! There are some people, though, that I truly want to mention here, because without them this book would not have been possible.

Melanie Abrahams, who I am so thankful to have met. Whose ability to get into my brain and help me write this book is like that of no other. Whose dedication, hard work, attention to detail, and research will make me always hold her in the highest regard, and to the many late evenings we spent together discussing this book and how to make it every pregnant woman's best companion.

Dr. Amos Grunebaum, whom I first met some 20-odd hours into the labor of my first son and whom I knew from that moment was the most competent, knowledgeable, and trustworthy doctor I could ever have had the great fortune to know. He has not only been the best obstetrician I could ever have dreamed for, but he has opened up his knowledge for me in this book and explained things in ways that I know will help generations of women have fulfilling, empowered, and healthier pregnancies.

Andrea Orbeck, whose commitment to health and fitness is unwavering and whose dedication to prenatal and postpartum wellness is inspiring. Just to know you makes me glow a little more, knowing that I am talking to someone who holds health in the highest regard.

Nanalee, my children's grandmother, whose constant support has given me the hours I needed to be able to write this book. It is so hard having to be away from my children, but knowing they are in the loving hands of their grandmother while I type away at the computer has made it all possible.

Brittany Hamblin, the most supportive editor I could have found. It is hard to have the confidence to finally put pen to paper, and knowing that Brittany is behind every one of those words, helping to get them to as many pregnant women as possible, fills me with confidence.

Alison Milam, for being a part of those early discussions when this book was still just a thought. You truly helped pull the knowledge out of me and put an end to all the procrastination.

Dina Light and my MomPrep staff, for constantly teaching me something new about the world of pregnancy and parenting.

Doctors, nurses, midwives, and health care professionals everywhere who care for pregnant women—your jobs are invaluable and your knowledge is inspiring. Thank you for helping us to bring healthy babies into the world every single day.

All of my clients, customers, and readers, who help me to never forget what it's like to be pregnant and what information you really want. I love all our candid conversations, emails, tweets, and Facebook posts, and I hope they keep coming for years and years to come.

And last but not least, I want to acknowledge all of the women and men who have struggled and continue to struggle to become parents. I have lived that journey and I know firsthand how heartbreaking it can be. I wish for every single one of you that you, too, will have a family one day and be able to read this book with joy. I will never stop thinking of you.

INDEX

To learn more about pregnancy, parenting, and style
and to shop Rosie Pope Maternity, visit me online at:

www.RosiePope.com/MommyIQBook